ᏬᏬᏬᏬᏬᏬᏬᏬᏬᏬᏬᏬᏬᏬᏬᏬᏬᏬᏬᏬᏬᏬ

How to Manage
Change Effectively

ᏬᏬᏬᏬᏬᏬᏬᏬᏬᏬᏬᏬᏬᏬᏬᏬᏬᏬᏬᏬᏬᏬ

Approaches, Methods,
and Case Examples

ഠ൦ഠ൦ഠ൦ഠ൦ഠ൦ഠ൦ഠ൦ഠ൦ഠ൦ഠ൦ഠ൦ഠ൦ഠ൦ഠ൦ഠ൦ഠ൦ഠ

Donald L. Kirkpatrick

ഠ൦ഠ൦ഠ൦ഠ൦ഠ൦ഠ൦ഠ൦ഠ൦ഠ൦ഠ൦ഠ൦ഠ൦ഠ൦ഠ൦ഠ൦ഠ൦ഠ

Foreword by Joe D. Batten

How to Manage Change Effectively

Jossey-Bass Publishers
San Francisco

HOW TO MANAGE CHANGE EFFECTIVELY
Approaches, Methods, and Case Examples
by Donald L. Kirkpatrick

Copyright © 1985 by: Jossey-Bass Inc., Publishers
350 Sansome Street
San Francisco, California 94104

Library of Congress Cataloging in Publication Data

Kirkpatrick, Donald L.
How to manage change effectively.

(The Jossey-Bass management series)
Bibliography: p. 273
Includes index.
1. Organizational change—Addresses, essays,
lectures. 2. Organizational effectiveness—Addresses,
essays, lectures. I. Title. II. Series.
HD58.8.K52   1985   658.4'06   85-45060
ISBN 0-87589-659-6

Manufactured in the United States of America

JACKET DESIGN BY WILLI BAUM

FIRST EDITION
HB Printing   10 9 8 7 6

Code 8536

The Jossey-Bass Management Series

Consulting Editors
Human Resources

Leonard Nadler
Zeace Nadler
College Park, Maryland

Foreword

A new book by Don Kirkpatrick is always a welcome event. He is that rare phenomenon, a "manager's manager" and an "educator's educator." In short, he brings to his audiences a rich amalgam of both theory and practice—that is, hands-on ways to move from concept to reality.

This book thoughtfully and succinctly explores how people *feel* about change, and how their motives, wants, needs, and possibilities affect their responses. Kirkpatrick's treatment of empathy as a key and crucial ingredient in preparing for and implementing change is realistic and useful.

He perceives communication as being central to all effective change and his definition of communication as "creating understanding" does much to illustrate why mere dialogue—two or more people engaged in monologues—is not enough. His treatment of listening and feedback is practical and cogent.

The third key component—participation—is perceived as a sought-after result of the first two. Without true involvement, there is no real commitment to change and all that it connotes.

Kirkpatrick emphasizes that change will always be with us and that it need not cause withdrawal or defensiveness. It should, rather, stimulate the kind of thinking, and planning of strategies and tactics, that make every day one of discovery, of zest and verve.

Kirkpatrick's wit enlivens his topic in ways we have come to expect from this master educator. But beyond that, this is a landmark work, a new standard in the vitally needed area of change management for a number of reasons.

First, it is comprehensive. It synthesizes the best from the works on this subject by Blake and Mouton, Odiorne, Hersey and Blanchard, Lippitt, Burack, Luthans, and Schaller. It presents philosophy, policies, procedures, practices, and processes for change. The impact of change on *all* the resources of an organization—the people, money, materials, time, and space—are examined and recommendations for absorbing that impact are provided. It offers guidance for the kind of involvement needed to ensure that commitments are pursued and executed with conviction. Feelings and reactions as well as strategies and tactics are accorded the significance due them.

Second, case studies of organizations like IBM, Xerox, International Minerals and Chemical Corporation, and Mercury Marine are served up in an enlightening and stimulating way. These case studies provide some very specific insights, some real do's and don't's.

Finally, this book is distinguished in that it provides a specific model for change. Again, Kirkpatrick's emphasis is on practicality. If your goal is to make changes in order to actualize possibilities for you and your organization in the future, this book is for you. Read it with a quickened feeling of confidence and discovery.

Des Moines, Iowa   Joe D. Batten
August 1985   *Chairman of the Board*
                                      Batten, Batten, Hudson,
                                      and Swab

CIO

Preface

It makes little difference whether your organization is big or small; old or new; service, manufacturing, or government; profit or nonprofit; located in the North, East, South, or West. Change is present. You can slow it down or accelerate it, but you can't stop it. It is there today and it will be there tomorrow and every day after tomorrow. And managers at every level are affected by change. Sometimes change is imposed from above. Sometimes there is pressure from subordinates to make changes. Sometimes managers have their own ideas for innovating in order to improve the effectiveness of their departments. In most organizations, no one has trained them in how to manage change, so they do the best they can, using their own philosophies and approaches. Sometimes they are successful, and sometimes they are not.

In reviewing the literature on change, I discovered many articles and books that present broad philosophical approaches that are of little or no help to practical managers. I found others that are practical and that offer suggestions and formulas for making decisions and getting them accepted. But none of them has put together a thorough understanding of the requirements for managing change effectively—a process that includes making decisions as well as getting them implemented with maximum acceptance.

This book was written specifically for managers in all types of organizations whose jobs are to implement ideas from top management as well as suggest and initiate ideas for improving the effectiveness and efficiency of their departments. In order to do their jobs effectively, managers need to understand both the science and art of managing change—which are defined by the Society for Advancement of Management (1980) as follows: "As a science, management is organized knowledge including concepts, theories, principles, and techniques underlying the practice of managing. As an art, it is the application of the organized knowledge to realities in a situation, usually with blend or compromise, to obtain desired practical results." Although each manager must provide the Art, this book will provide the Science.

In *How to Manage Change Effectively,* concepts and principles are supplemented by practical advice on what to do and how to do it. This book provides answers to the following types of questions that managers are asking:

- How will my subordinates react to a change that I think is a good idea?
- How can I get change accepted by my subordinates?
- How fast should I try to implement a change that's been decided on?
- What do I do if my boss asks me to make a change that I think is a mistake?
- Should I go to my boss with an idea for a change or should I go ahead and make the change and tell the boss afterward?
- What if my boss says no to a change I recommend?
- What should I do if a change isn't working out?
- Should I suggest change to managers in other departments or should I "mind my own business"?
- How much should I involve my subordinates when deciding on a change?
- How much should I involve my subordinates when implementing a change?
- How far ahead should I communicate a change?

This book will be of interest and help to professionals in human resource development (HRD). This includes personnel managers, training directors, and managers of human resources, who often function as change agents and also assist in managing change. In addition, they conduct conferences and seminars to teach the management of change. The concepts, principles, and techniques described in this book can provide the basis for such training courses; indeed, they do just that for me in the numerous seminars I conduct on managing change. This book will also help HRD professionals work with managers on a one-on-one basis to help them achieve changes in their departments.

In order to include a thorough knowledge of how to manage change, I have drawn on two sources. Chapter Three contains summaries of twelve publications that offer practical information dealing with change and how to manage it. The case studies in Part Three of the book represent the other source of ideas. All of the cases are real. Most of them were written especially for this book.

Part One deals with philosophy and principles. Chapter One describes many changes currently taking place that range from automating sheep shearing in Australia to the use of computers in American-made automobiles. The three roles that managers play are identified in Chapter Two. The first role is to implement changes that are decided on from higher management; the second is to recommend changes to higher management and ask for approval; the third is to initiate changes without asking for approval from higher management. A clear description is provided regarding the factors that determine whether changes should be recommended or initiated. The third chapter summarizes previously written articles and books dealing with philosophy, principles, and methods for implementing change. A common recommendation is the need for managers to involve subordinates in the changes that will affect them. Chapter Four details the reasons why some people resent or resist change while others accept or welcome it. Some of the more common reasons for resenting or resisting are fear of personal loss, lack of input to those making the decision, and lack of respect for those deciding on the change. Some of the main reasons for accepting or welcoming include personal gain from the decision, clear understanding of the reasons for the change, and respect and trust for those making the decision.

Part Two describes specific approaches and methods for

making change decisions and getting them accepted. Chapter Five describes a seven-step model for instituting changes successfully. It includes a discussion of the need for communication and participation. Chapters Six, Seven, and Eight identify the three keys that will result in the effective management of change. Chapter Six stresses the need for empathy; that is, for determining how people will react to the change. Chapter Seven describes ways to communicate the change to the people it will affect. And Chapter Eight provides insight into how and when to get input from those who will be affected by the change. Chapter Nine contains two case examples that illustrate the application of the principles and approaches described in chapters Six, Seven, and Eight.

Part Three presents nine case examples of organizations that have successfully planned and implemented changes. Some of the cases describe office situations, including the implementation of a new personnel policy to allow variable working hours. Others describe factory situations, including the planning and implementation of quality circles. A brief summary of each case example is provided at the beginning of Part Three so readers can easily choose those cases that relate to their own specific problems or interests.

A final chapter summarizes the most significant parts of the book to help the reader with immediate application.

In order to stimulate and challenge the reader, a pretest and posttest are included. Readers are encouraged to complete the pretest before reading the book. The pretest allows readers to assess their own philosophies and knowledge. It also alerts readers to the main issues I address. The posttest is to be completed after reading the book. By comparing pretest and posttest responses and scores, readers can see what changes have occurred in their knowledge and attitudes.

The ideas expressed in this book have come from many sources over a period of more than ten years of studying and teaching the subject of managing change.

Many of my ideas and insights have developed as a result of discussions with friends and colleagues in the three organizations in which I've been most active. Many thanks to those of you who have touched my life at the Management Institute of the University of Wisconsin Extension, the American Society for Training and Development, and Elmbrook Church.

I am grateful to the authors who provided the content for Chapter Three. I am also grateful to the following authors who contributed case studies: Peter Land, James Ehrenstrom, Milford Jacobsen, Lynn Bardele, Roy Walters, Sud Ingle, Robert Blake, Jane Mouton, Richard McCarthy, R. C. Brown, W. W. Castor, and Edward Jones.

I appreciate the stimulating influence that Joe D. Batten has had on me through his books, films, and teaching, and extend my thanks for his graciously agreeing to write the Foreword.

I would also like to acknowledge the helpful suggestions I received from Leonard and Zeace Nadler. They were able to suggest major changes to improve the book.

I owe a great deal of thanks to Linda Smith, my program assistant, who demonstrated a rare combination of ability and patience in reading my writing and typing and retyping as I kept revising the manuscript.

Finally, I want to thank the good Lord who gave me my wife, Fern. During our thirty-five years of marriage, we have been through many changes, including the raising of four wonderful children. Her constant love and encouragement have been an inspiration to me. I dedicate this book to her.

Milwaukee, Wisconsin   Donald L. Kirkpatrick
August 1985

Contents

The Author

Donald L. Kirkpatrick is professor of management at the Management Institute, University of Wisconsin. He received his B.A. degree (1948) in accounting, his M.B.A. degree (1949) in personnel management, and his Ph.D. degree (1954) in personnel guidance and counseling, all from the University of Wisconsin at Madison.

Kirkpatrick served as training supervisor with International Minerals and Chemical Corporation (1960-1962) and as personnel manager with Bendix Corporation (1962-1964). He received the Research Award from the American Society for Personnel Administration in 1969, the Distinguished Service Award from the University of Wisconsin-Extension in 1976, the Best Book of the Year Award from the American Society for Personnel Administration in 1982, and the Gordon M. Bliss Memorial Award as the outstanding trainer from the American Society for Training and Development in 1983. He has been a member of the Board of Directors of the American Society for Personnel Administration (1962-1964) and national president of the American Society for Training and Development (1975).

Kirkpatrick has published numerous articles in such periodicals as the *Journal of Training and Development, Personnel Administrator, Personnel Journal,* and *Personnel.* His published books include *How to Plan and Conduct Productive Business Meetings* (1976); *How to Select and Train New First-Line Supervisors* (1980, with Coverdale and Olsen-Tjensvold); *How to*

Improve Performance Through Appraisal and Coaching (1982);
No-Nonsense Communication, third edition (1983); and *Supervisory Training and Development,* second edition (1983). He
has also published seven Supervisory/Management Inventories
including "Management Inventory on Managing Change."

His speaking and consulting work has taken him to Mexico, Brazil, India, Australia, Singapore, Hong Kong, Toyko, and
Taiwan.

How to Manage Change Effectively

Approaches, Methods, and Case Examples

Pretest:
A Self-Assessment
of Change Management
Knowledge

The following pretest should be completed before reading the book. It was designed to stimulate the reader's interest and to measure the level of knowledge of the concepts and principles that are described in the book. Before reading the book, answer each item with *A* to indicate you agree or *D* to indicate that you disagree with the statement. The test should be scored by using the author's answers that are found on page 263.

The same test is found on page 258, there called the "posttest," to be completed after reading the book. This should also be scored by comparing the answers given on page 263. A comparison of pretest and posttest scores and responses will give some indication of the amount of learning that has taken place by reading the book. Incorrect responses on the posttest will challenge the reader to take another look at certain parts of the book.

In analyzing responses and scores, it is important to recognize that the answers are not "true" or "false." Rather, the "agree" and "disagree" responses demonstrate that the "correct" answers are the opinions of the author based on his experience, education, and philosophy.

1

Pretest

Insert *A* (agree) or *D* (disagree) in front of each question to indicate your opinion.

_____ 1. Your boss has decided on a change that you feel would be a mistake. You should go ahead and implement it without challenging it.

_____ 2. Managers should constantly be looking for changes that will improve department efficiency and/or morale.

_____ 3. If you were promoted to a management job, you should make the job different than it was under your predecessor.

_____ 4. "You can't argue with success."

_____ 5. People doing a particular job are one of the best sources of ideas to improve that job.

_____ 6. Very few people in any department have any ideas to improve the effectiveness of the department or the organization.

_____ 7. In order to get a large number of suggestions from people, you must give money or prizes for ideas that are accepted and implemented.

_____ 8. Managers should freely suggest changes to managers in other departments.

_____ 9. Most managers would welcome ideas and suggestions from people in other departments.

_____ 10. Managers should welcome ideas and suggestions from all sources.

_____ 11. If you think a change should be made in your department, you should always ask your boss for approval before making the change.

_____ 12. If changes do not have any impact on other departments, you should implement the changes without bothering to clear them with your boss.

_____ 13. If a change doesn't cost any money, you should implement it without bothering to clear it with your boss.

——— 14. The style of leadership of the boss is the most important factor to consider when managers are trying to decide whether to recommend or initiate a change.

——— 15. Bosses and subordinates should have an understanding regarding the kinds of changes that can be implemented by the subordinate without getting prior approval from the boss.

——— 16. You should encourage your subordinates to try out any changes that they feel should be made.

——— 17. If your boss says no to a change you've recommended, you should forget about it.

——— 18. The quality of a decision based on facts and logic is more important than the acceptance of those who must carry it out.

——— 19. Changes based on facts and logic can be sabotaged, intentionally or not, by persons affected by the change.

——— 20. If you are planning to make a radical change in your department, you should secretly gather facts, prepare your final plans, and sell those people affected on the basis of facts and logic.

——— 21. In order to save time and be decisive, a manager should make decisions regarding change without seeking input from subordinates.

——— 22. Decisions to change should be based on opinions as well as facts.

——— 23. Managers should always maintain the authority to make the final decision when they ask for input from subordinates.

——— 24. If subordinates participate in the decision to make a change, they are usually more enthusiastic in carrying it out.

——— 25. If a change has been implemented and it isn't working out as expected, the change should be rescinded and the old way should be reinstated.

——— 26. You've decided on a change and announced it. You then receive more data and now know it's a mistake. You should retract the decision and apologize for the mistake.

____ 27. When you've decided on a change and announced it to your subordinates, you should never retract it even if it is not well received.

____ 28. People with negative attitudes toward change should be encouraged to quit.

____ 29. If one subordinate enthusiastically resists a change, you should clamp down hard on that person so the other subordinates won't do the same thing.

____ 30. People will automatically accept changes decided on by experts.

____ 31. You should tell your subordinates as far in advance as practical about a change that will affect them.

____ 32. People should be informed in advance of unpleasant changes as well as pleasant changes.

____ 33. If a change is going to be resisted no matter what you do, there is no point in communicating the reasons for the change.

____ 34. If a change is going to result in the termination of one or more people, this should be made clear before the change is implemented.

____ 35. You should do everything you can to find other jobs for people whose jobs are eliminated by a change.

____ 36. It's a good idea to sell a change to the natural leader among your subordinates before trying to sell it to the others.

____ 37. It is usually better to communicate with a group concerning a change than to talk to each person individually.

____ 38. Explaining the reasons for a change will always turn resistance into acceptance.

____ 39. Logical explanation by a manager will not be accepted if the feelings of the subordinates are ignored.

____ 40. If a change is introduced at the right time, by the right person, in the right manner, it will always be accepted.

_____ 41. People who don't understand the reasons for a change will always resist it.

_____ 42. People are always anxious to move from an old office to a new one.

_____ 43. People are always anxious to have new equipment to work with.

_____ 44. Some people are not anxious to be promoted to a job with more responsibility.

_____ 45. One of the most frequent reasons why employees resent and/or resist change is the fear they might lose something.

_____ 46. The timing of a change can be very important in its acceptance.

_____ 47. Before making a change, managers should determine to what extent subordinates will accept the change.

_____ 48. Once you've decided on a change, you should implement it immediately.

_____ 49. Most people will accept a change if managers explain that the change is necessary for the survival of the organization.

_____ 50. When a change has been decided on, it is a good idea to get subordinates involved in helping you implement the change.

Part I

OIOIOIOIOIOIOIOIOIOIOIOIOIOIOIOIOIOIOIOIOIOIO

Approaches to Managing Change

OIOIOIOIOIOIOIOIOIOIOIOIOIOIOIOIOIOIOIOIOIOIO

Part One is designed to provide readers with an understanding of some underlying philosophy and principles before methods and techniques for managing change are addressed later in the book.

Chapter One illustrates through examples that changes are constantly taking place, some of which create employee problems that managers must face. One of the main changes deals with the computer and automation. Other common changes concern reorganization, working conditions, personnel policies, and philosophies of management. All of these require managers to consider carefully how they can get them accepted by the people who are affected.

Chapter Two describes the three roles that managers should play in dealing with change. The first is to implement changes decided on by higher management. If the manager feels that such a change is good, he or she should carry it out. If, however, the manager feels that the change is a mistake, he or she should question it, give reasons for opposing it, and offer a counter-suggestion. Managers also need to perform the roles of recommending and initiating change. In both roles, the manager

7

decides on a change, usually with input from subordinates. When a manager feels that a change should be made, he or she must decide whether to recommend it to the boss for approval or initiate it without checking with the boss. This chapter describes the important considerations a manager must face in making the decision.

Chapter Three presents the change philosophy, principles, and approaches of twelve authors affiliated with business, universities, and consulting organizations. Themes that are common to most of their works include the need to understand people, communicate effectively, and elicit involvement from those who will be affected by the change.

Chapter Four provides insight into the reasons why some people accept and even welcome change while others resent or resist it. It expodes the myth that everybody resists change. For example, it describes how some people resist a change because they are fearful of losing such things as status, authority, self-satisfaction, money, and even job security. At the same time, other people look at the change and welcome it, usually because they feel they will gain the things that others feel they will lose. Other reasons for negative and positive reactions are also described.

These four chapters provide a necessary background to understanding the methods and techniques that are described in Part Two.

1

οιοιοιοιοιοιοιοιοιοιοιοιοιοιοιοιοιοιοιοιο

The Changes Managers Face

The word *change* strikes fear into the minds and hearts of some people. To others, it brings a ray of hope. And this condition will exist until the end of time.

There's no way to avoid it. Changes are going to take place, probably at an increasing rate. Everyone is affected. It is happening in every industry and business. It is happening in every governmental organization and in every home. And those who are in charge must know how to decide on changes and implement them effectively or they will fail. The principles for doing it are quite simple. The application of the principles is not so easy.

Examples of Change

In recent years, the introduction and modification of the computer has dominated the list of changes occurring. It has affected nearly every medium and large business and industry. It is currently affecting small business, churches, and homes. It won't quit but will continue to affect the lives of more and more people. For example, a recent article in the *Wall Street Journal* (1984) described the rapid change in the home-buying process: "Looking 30 years down the road, housing experts see a national housing market rather than the traditional local market. They predict that computers will offer information about homes nationwide and that computer processing will put a house in its new owner's hands in one or two days instead of the usual six to eight weeks. Along the way, financial service

9

networks will mushroom until the real estate agent and the banker melt into one, providing home buyers with one-stop shopping."

A dramatic change that will affect nearly everyone is taking place in the automobile industry. In fact, computerized autos aren't just around the corner; they are here. The first prototype, a Buick Riviera with a video display terminal (VDT), was available in May 1984 on an experimental basis. According to plans, 5,000 screen-equipped Rivieras will be offered for sale in 1985. Full-color displays will soon be available and by 1987, such cathode ray terminals (CRTs) will be standard on most top-of-the-line autos. Owners will be able to use "soft switches" as well as voice to tell the computerized equipment what to do. And if the driver has a question, he or she may get an answer from the voice that's been programmed into the equipment. Ford has even spent a lot of money deciding whether to use a male or female voice. The preference was to use a male voice because it was more appealing.

Automation is occurring at an ever-increasing rate. For example, Australia is trying to automate sheep shearing. A recent article (*Plain Dealer,* 1983) described it as follows:

> *Melbourne, Australia*—Mary had a little lamb, its fleece was white as snow, and everywhere that Mary went, her lamb was being measured, tested, prodded by machines, injected with chemicals or slapped into production lines to have its wool shorn by robots. No one is really going to rewrite the old nursery rhyme, but if scientists and engineers here get their way, sheep shearers, the romantic nomads of the wide-open Australian bush may become as quaint as Little Bo Peep. Imagine for a moment a pen full of fluffy white sheep. A pair of steel fingers reaches into the pen and, one by one, plucks out the sheep, slapping them onto a conveyor that parades them like so many car bodies past a fleece-clipping robot. Or picture sheep being fed or sprayed or injected with substances that enable handlers to defrock a flock in minutes by pulling the fleece off by hand or sucking it up with a vacuum.
>
> Researchers at Australian universities and gov-

ernment laboratories are experimenting with these and other novel approaches to separate sheep from their coats, one of the most difficult but essential tasks in a country that has nine times as many sheep as men.

"The wool industry has a need to reduce costs like all other industries," said Peter Austin, spokesman for Australian Wool Corp., a government body that spends about $2 million annually on research programs aimed at developing cheaper and more efficient ways of harvesting wool. Technical gains in other industries haven't come to the wool industry. In fact, there has not been a significant practical improvement in shearing technology since 1868, when a patent was issued for a kind of automatic razor powered by steam, compressed air or water-driven turbine. Before that, sheep had been fleeced with hand-powered shears.

Wickham Skinner of the Harvard Business School told the *New York Times* that right now there are probably about two dozen fully integrated high-technology "factories of the future" in the United States. It will probably take ten years or so for the concept of the fully automated factory to diffuse widely. But in the meantime, management is investing heavily in such advanced production technologies as robots, laser scanners, supersonic welding, ultrasonic probes, and other methods that were little used only a short while ago. The typical job is no longer characterized by great physical effort and repetitive tasks. Workers mainly monitor and maintain automated machinery, repair errors detected by automatic sensors, and perform final assembly. The workers need not keep pace with a continuously moving line but control the advance of the workpiece by pulling a handle.

In Japan, the Yamazaki Machinery Works plant is the state of the art in flexible manufacturing systems. It is billed as the first factory in the world that can be run on the phone. It starts with computer-aided design (CAD); then the numerically controlled machines take over. What 195 workers needed ninety conventional machines and five weeks to accomplish, they can now do in three days with 40 workers. Based on its success, the company developed the MAZATROL program, which is now available in nine languages. The union in Missan was concerned about automation and its impact on the security of employees. In 1983, they negotiated a contract in which management promised (1) no high-technology equipment would be installed without consulting the union first, (2) any replaced workers would not be fired, laid off, or paid less, and (3) transferred workers would be retrained for new jobs appropriate to their abilities and aptitudes.

Changes are constantly being made to keep us healthy. For example, a recent article appeared in the *Journal of the Wisconsin Dental Association* (Tyre and Bojar, 1980, p. 633) that described "New Techniques for the Management of the Anxious Dental Patient": "It is well known that dental disease is a widespread source of distress. As is true in many applied fields of medicine, technology seems to have provided an ample supply of resources for the treatment of disease, and the issue has increasingly become one of getting our patients to comply with what we know to be health-sustaining behavior. Efficient new techniques address the two principle factors interfering with routine dental care: *pain* and *fear* regarding dentistry. There are many patients who are quite fearful of the injection procedures required in the use of local anesthetics. Alternative treatments tend to be anxiety reducing techniques, involving biofeedback, assisted muscle relaxation, behavioral deconditioning for anxiety, and, in select cases, pain management procedures involving hypnosis."

A recent newspaper article described a transportation change at the famous Inca settlement called Machu Picchu in Peru. Tourists are transported by bus from the bottom of the hill to the top and back again. Those of us who have been there remember the young boy, about ten years of age, who runs straight down the hill and yells and waves at the tourists in the bus as it zigs back and forth down the steep incline. At the bottom of the hill, the boy is standing by the door of the bus as the tourists exit. Nearly all the tourists give the boy a tip as he smiles with his hand out. (He probably makes more money than the bus driver.) When the bus is unloaded, the boy hops in and rides back to the top. A cable car will be installed to transport tourists up and down the hill. It will replace the bus drivers, unless they can be trained to operate the cable car. It will certainly replace the boy who has made a good living for himself and probably his family. And tourists will miss the joy of watching and tipping the boy.

Another common change is the reorganization of many companies. Conglomerates are absorbing more and more organizations, with or without their consent. Sometimes drastic changes are forced on the organization being absorbed. Executives from the larger organization may replace those from the one that was taken over. Policies of the parent company may be imposed on the organization that has been absorbed. If no changes are immediately made, people at all levels are expecting them and are reacting positively or negatively in anticipation. Perhaps the changes will come and perhaps they won't.

Working conditions change. Many organizations have built or remodeled their facilities and people are asked (or told) to move into new quarters. For example, Sears and Standard Oil of Indiana moved many people from old offices to their tall buildings in the heart of the Loop of downtown Chicago. This required many changes in transportation and other aspects of the job.

Policies, procedures, and rules are frequently changed. A well-known Milwaukee organization, for example, recently changed its policy regarding the drinking of coffee on the job. Other organizations have made changes regarding vacations, benefits, smoking, wash-up time, punching a time clock, working hours, hiring, promotions, retirement, and dress. Typically, the policy changes have been decided on by top management and communicated through the personnel department. Personnel departments are finding that the new policy may be better, and certainly better accepted, if a task force of line managers develop the change. Harnischfeger Corporation of Milwaukee, for example, is using this approach to develop a new policy regarding smoking.

The role of women in society has seen some drastic changes, not only in the United States but over much of the world. Following is a feature story that appeared in a Singapore paper (*Straits Times,* 1983).

> Over a period of time, many things change and bring with them new features. The effects of changing times are not limited to the environment alone. They also involve human lives, men and women.
>
> One aspect of change we can easily identify in the Malay women in Singapore is with regard to working life. In the past they were known to have spent more time behind the kitchen doors; but today almost 50 percent of Malay women are working. Many work in the factories as production operators while some are postwomen and office workers. A few are nurses, teachers, principals, journalists, lawyers, and doctors. Although the number of Malay women professionals is still very small, they do affect the social life and awareness of the Malays.
>
> The role of women as the "backbone" of daily family living is being threatened. This is the result of women having to divide the little time they have between the many pieces of work they have to do and their family commitments. The effect is seriously felt. Because of work, household chores can no longer be done as good as they used to be. The same effect can also be noticed in how present-day women take care of their growing children. This, however, does not mean that working life has made Malay women a less important party in the affairs of their families. Their importance, as women and as human beings, still remains the same but the "fields" in which they play important roles have changed. Previously, husbands were the sole breadwinners in their families. But today, this is no longer the case in many families.

A change in management is an everyday occurrence. Sometimes a manager is replaced because of promotion, retirement, or death. At other times, he or she is fired. The replacement may come from inside or outside an organization. If from the inside, the replacement may come from inside or outside the department. Sometimes, there is no change in the individual who is the manager but only in the style of leadership that he or she provides. Books are written and management seminars are constantly being offered with one objective in mind—to change the behavior of the manager. For example, a manager who used to be concerned only with production has been trained to be equally concerned with the morale of employees. He or she is taught skills of motivation instead of relying on threats and fear.

"Concession bargaining" is being used by many organizations in negotiating contracts with a union. The old approach where the company simply reacted to "union demands" has been replaced by management asking (or demanding) certain concessions from the union. Real negotiations are taking place in an atmosphere of give-and-take. Some union leaders refer to it as "union-busting tactics" but go along with it because of the fear that companies will either move or go out of business.

Employees of today are typically very different from employees of twenty or thirty years ago, primarily in regard to attitude. They seem to have less respect for authority and want to be asked and persuaded rather than simply told what to do. They also want their ideas to be listened to, considered, and hopefully used. Many of them want more freedom in doing their jobs. And they thereby provide more of a challenge to the managers. Some managers accept this change and manage accordingly, while others go around moaning, "They don't make workers like they used to!"

A major change in philosophy has taken place in many organizations. It started with "management by objectives" where managers were persuaded and trained to have subordinates help to set their own objectives. It has expanded to become "participative management" where subordinates become a more important part of all decisions. Specific programs such as "quality of work life," "quality circles," and "performance circles" have been introduced in many organizations in order to be sure that participation becomes a reality and not just a philosophy. IBM developed an approach called PRIDE, which stands for "People Responsibly Involved Developing Excellence." A division of Goodyear has called it "EI," which simply means "employee involvement." The president tells his managers to do it but leaves the choice and techniques for implementing the program

to them. Four assumptions underlie these participative programs:

1. People who do the work are best qualified to improve it.
2. Decision making should be pushed down to the lowest level
    possible.
3. Worker participation increases both job satisfaction and
    commitment to company objectives.
4. There is a vast pool of ideas in the work force waiting to be
    tapped.

One of the most amusing changes relates to a famous pro-
nouncement by Jonathan Swift, "You can't make a silk purse
out of a sow's ear." The *National Geographic* of January 1984
announced that Arthur D. Little, a management consulting organization actually did in 1921 in Cambridge, Massachusetts.
The silk purse is now in a vault in the Smithsonian Museum in
Washington, D.C.

The Future

What will the future be like? We know it will be different
but in what ways? At a recent meeting of human resource executives, Philip Farish, editor of *Industrial Relations News* (IRN)
presented a profile of human resources for the year 2000 (*Behavioral Sciences Newsletter,* 1983a). He reported the results of
a Delphi forecasting process conducted by IRN among association executives and consultants serving a cross section of business and industry. The purpose was to develop a convergence of
opinion on significant trends in human resources as well as its
social, technological, and economic context. Although opinion
among participants was not unanimous, here are some of the
trends that were identified.

Organizational Characteristics

- Organizations and management systems will become more
  complex.
- Demand for productivity improvement will come from high
  business costs, not popular pressure.

- Younger workers will find their advancement blocked by older workers and will need special motivational action through task forces, lateral transfers, and similar measures.
- Pressure will continue for better working conditions, more participation, and due process.
- Growth of video terminals and electronic mail will continue.
- Average workweek will be shorter, and alternative schedules will be more common.
- Many semiskilled jobs will be eliminated by robots and numerically controlled tools.

Training and Development

- Employers will feel increasing pressure to provide training in entry-level skills.
- Fast technological change will call for more training and retraining.
- Management development will be more important to keep managers up-to-date and to motivate them as advancement gets harder.

General Personnel Administration

- Personnel's position in the corporate hierarchy will be determined by involvement in strategic planning.
- Promotion, transfer, and separation of employees will become more complicated.
- Outplacement will become routine.
- Employee communications will become less paternal in tone.
- In labor-management relations, more attention will go toward developing greater collaboration.
- Occupational health will dominate safety/health considerations.
- Personnel's function will include matters related to the organization's mission: interpreting the effect of technical developments on the human aspects of the system; interpreting social and political pressures from outside which can effect the organization's pursuit of its mission; collaborating on interpretation of human systems and technical systems.

When is it all going to end? When are we going to keep

things as they are? Or better yet, when are we going to get back to the "good old days"? And what is meant by "the good old days"? Here's one description (Geiger, 1872):

The "Good Old Days"
Rules and Regulations

1. Office employees will daily sweep the floors, dust the furniture, shelves, and showcases.
2. Each day fill lamps, clean chimneys, and trim wicks. Wash the windows once a week.
3. Each clerk will bring in a bucket of water and a scuttle of coal for the day's business.
4. Make your pens carefully. You may whittle nibs to your individual taste.
5. This office will open at 7 A.M. and close at 8 P.M. daily except on the Sabbath, on which day it will remain closed.
6. Men employees will be given an evening off each week for courting purposes, or two evenings a week if they go regularly to church.
7. Every employee should lay aside from each pay a goodly sum of his earnings for his benefits during his declining, so that he will not become a burden upon the charity of his betters.
8. Any employee who smokes Spanish cigars, uses liquor in any form, gets shaved at a barber shop, or frequents pool or public halls will give a good reason to suspect his worth, intentions, integrity, and honesty.
9. The employee who has performed his labors faithfully and without faults for a period of five years in my service and who has been thrifty and attentive to his religious duties is looked upon by his fellow men as a substantial and law-abiding citizen and will be given an increase of five cents per day, providing a just return of profits from the business permits it.

The answer to "when is it going to end?" is obvious. Never! Today it's time for a change. And tomorrow it's time for another change. Therefore, managers need to understand this fact and learn how to manage change so that the right decisions will be made as well as be accepted by the employees.

2

oIoIoIoIoIoIoIoIoIoIoIoIoIoIoIoIoIoIoIoIoIoIoIo

The Manager's Role

Managers at all levels from first-line supervisor to chief executive officer have three important roles to play. Their first role is to implement changes that come from higher management. The other two roles have to do with changes that they think should be made. Ideas for these changes come from many sources including themselves, their subordinates, and their peers in other departments. The roles they have to decide on are whether to recommend the change to the boss or to go ahead and initiate the change without getting approval from the boss.

Implement Changes from Above

If a manager is told to make a change and he or she feels it is a good change, it is easy to carry out the change enthusiastically. But if the manager thinks that the change is a bad change, he or she must know how to act.

Some managers feel that they must implement the change whether they like it or not. They feel this way either because they are afraid to alienate the boss or because they want to be a "loyal" employee (and also a long-term employee!). If the manager thinks the change is a mistake (that is, will cause more problems than it's worth), he or she should first of all ask, "Why is the change being recommended?" It is obvious that higher management has a reason—and it's a good reason to them —why the change should be made. If the manager understands the reason or reasons, he or she may agree that it's a good change.

19

But suppose the manager still feels it is a bad change. What then? The manager should "challenge" the change. Some managers don't feel that they should do this. One reason is that some bosses don't like to be challenged by subordinates. Perhaps a clarification of the word *challenge* is needed. It means that the manager will express his or her thoughts to the boss—tactfully, of course. He or she will tell why the change is thought to be a mistake and what problems it will cause, as well as offer a recommendation on what to do. The "what to do" might be to leave things the way they are or to make a change different from the one decided on by higher management. This is truly being "loyal" to the organization.

But what if higher management says, "Thanks for your input. The decision has been made, so get going and do it!" Then what should the subordinate manager do? At this point, there are four choices.

1. Insist that higher management is wrong and that they should change their minds and do what the subordinate manager says.
2. Quit.
3. Carry out the change with as much enthusiasm as he or she can muster.
4. Carry out the change but tell his or her subordinates such things as "I told them it was a mistake but they wouldn't listen!" or "We'll have to do it even though we know it's a mistake."

In the book *Up the Organization* (Townsend, 1970, p. 53), the following procedure was suggested by Napoleon: "any commander in chief (manager) who undertakes to carry out a plan which he considers defective is at fault; he must put forward his reasons, insist on the plan being changed, and finally tender his resignation rather than be the instrument of his army's (organization's) downfall."

In one organization where I presented this philosophy, one of the foremen said, "If I *insist* on the plan being changed, I won't even get a chance to resign!"

The best choice of the four alternatives is probably the third one. In order to drum up some enthusiasm, the manager must understand and accept the reasons why higher management decided on the change. Even if he or she feels it will cause problems in the department, the broader reasons for the change should be stressed. For example, many managers rightfully feel that the introduction or extended use of the computer will cause problems. They must accept the fact that the computer is necessary even if it will create more work for them. And they must implement the decision by following the required procedures. Their job is to be as enthusiastic as possible and gain acceptance from subordinates.

When I was personnel manager of a large multidivision company, the general manager was paid a visit by three executives from the corporate office. They suggested a change in organizational structure from a strictly functional organization, as shown in Figure 1(a), to one that emphasized the two major products, as shown in Figure 1(b).

The conversation between the general manager (G.M.) and the corporate executives (C.E.) went something like this:

G.M.: Gentlemen, what can I do for you?

C.E.: We have a suggestion that we feel will make your operation more profitable.

G.M.: Good, we can stand that. What is your suggestion?

C.E.: We've been making a study of various types of organizations and we would like to suggest a slight change in your functional organization.

G.M.: What do you suggest?

C.E.: We have been working with some of our other divisions and have helped them modify their organizations. The results have been very good.

G.M.: What do you suggest?

C.E.: Well, we suggest that you have an assistant general manager in charge of each of your two major products. Both of these assistant general managers would report to you.

G.M.: Who would report to them?

Figure 1. Organizational Structure Change.

(a) *Organization by Function.*

(b) *Organization by Product.*

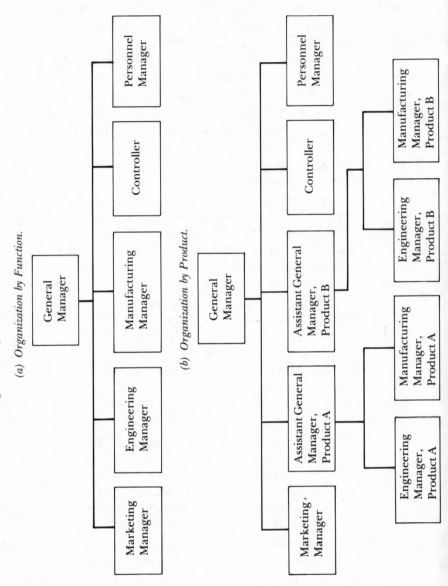

C.E.:	Both engineering and manufacturing would report to them instead of to you, but marketing, finance, and personnel would still report directly to you.
G.M.:	You know that I considered that when I set up this division. But I felt that the functional organization would work better.
C.E.:	You'd still have the same number of people reporting to you. The only change would be that engineering and manufacturing would report directly to the assistant general manager in charge of that product. This would provide more coordination and cooperation between engineering and manufacturing and also better control.
G.M.:	I'm not worried about how many people report to me. I'm concerned about productivity and profitability. My engineering manager and manufacturing manager are doing a very good job and I feel that the present structure is better than the one you suggest.
C.E.:	We've done a lot of research on this—both inside and outside our organization—and we feel strongly that the change would improve both productivity and profitability.
G.M.:	Well, I don't think so. Thanks for your suggestion, but I'd like to continue with the present organization structure.
C.E.:	(after a long pause) We've tried to present this to you in a nice way but apparently you don't buy it.
G.M.:	That is correct.
C.E.:	Well—we represent the president of the corporation and we've been authorized to make the decision that the structure of this division will be as we've suggested.
G.M.:	Is that final?
C.E.:	Yes, it is.
G.M.:	What options do I have?
C.E.:	You can stay as general manager under the new structure and we'll work with you to pick the two assistant general managers.
G.M.:	Or?
C.E.:	I guess we'll have to find a new general manager.

G.M.:   Where would that leave me?

C.E.:   We'd give you six months to find a job with another organization. We'd provide you with an office during that
period.

G.M.:   (after a short pause) I hate to give up seventeen years
with an organization that has treated me so well, but I
guess I'll have to do it. I feel that you are suggesting—or
rather *ordering*—a change that I can't accept.

C.E.:   We are sorry you feel this way and the organization is
going to miss you. But if that's your decision, we'll
have to accept it.

This true story is quite unusual in the fact that the general
manager felt so strongly about the decision that he resigned. In
most instances, the general manager would probably have swal-
lowed a little pride and accepted the change—at least for the
time being.

Recommend or Initiate Changes

A manager shouldn't wait for changes to be handed down
from higher management. Rather, he or she should be constantly searching for changes to improve departmental productivity
as well as morale. The idea can come from many sources, especially subordinates. When the manager has an idea that should
be implemented, he or she has a choice between recommending
it to the boss or implementing it without asking for approval.

There are a number of factors for a manager to consider in
deciding whether to recommend it to the boss in order to get
approval or to initiate the change without consulting the boss.
These factors include the leadership style of the boss, possible
impact on other departments, financial considerations, policies
and rules, and courage.

The *leadership style of the boss* is the most significant factor for a manager to consider when deciding whether to recommend a change to the boss or to go ahead and initiate it. Some
bosses reserve the decision-making process for themselves. Subordinates have not been given the authority to make changes.

Their job is to recommend and the boss makes that clear. He or she may have adopted this leadership style for several reasons. One reason is that he or she doesn't trust subordinates to made decisions. This feeling could be based on past experience where subordinates have made bad decisions and the boss has been "burned." Or it could be based on the assumption that the present subordinates don't have the knowledge or ability to make sound decisions. Another possible reason for this leadership style is philosophical. Bosses are paid to make decisions. They are accountable for their decisions. Their job is to make decisions and they may feel it is wrong to delegate this authority and responsibility to subordinates. A third possible reason is the fact that no one has suggested any other approach. Subordinates have always come to them with recommendations and they have said yes or no. They haven't even given thought to any other style.

The opposite style of leadership is exhibited by managers who have developed a philosophy and practice of giving subordinates the decision-making responsibility and authority. They may do it because they feel that better decisions can be made by subordinates who are closer to the situation. Or, they may do it because they don't want to be bothered by subordinates who constantly come to them and ask, "What should I do?" Or, they may have read the famous article called "Management Time: Who's Got the Monkey?" (Oncken and Wass, 1974) and have decided to keep the "monkey" (the problem) on the back of the subordinate. Or, they may recognize that people who make their own decisions are usually more enthusiastic and committed in carrying out the decision. Finally, they may feel that subordinates must learn to make decisions by doing it and living with the consequences.

Obviously, some managers take neither extreme. They carefully determine how much decision-making authority they want to give to each subordinate. In some cases, especially where the subordinate is new to the job or has a record of poor decisions, the boss will require subordinates to recommend instead of initiate changes. In other cases, especially where the subordinate has proven his or her ability to make decisions or where the risk of a poor decision is worth the possible benefits, the boss will encourage subordinates to initiate rather than recommend.

Another factor that helps determine whether a manager should recommend or initiate a change is the *significance of the change*. If it doesn't cost any money or is within the budget, the tendency is to initiate the change. The same is true if it doesn't involve any other departments. If, however, it would cost a lot of money or be outside the budget, approval may be needed from the boss before making the change. Or, if the change will affect other departments, it is better to recommend it so that the implications can be studied at a higher level.

Let's suppose, for example, that a manager feels it is a good idea to introduce variable or flexible working hours into the department. He or she would ask all employees what working hours they would prefer and would then make the decision based on the needs of the department as well as the wishes of each individual. On the surface it seems to be a departmental decision, but a closer look would indicate that it would have an effect on other departments where employees would go to their managers and demand the same policy. The personnel department would have a "tiger by the tail" to try to establish a policy in order to keep everyone happy. (See the case study in Chapter Eleven that describes how a large insurance company implemented such a policy.)

Another factor that helps to determine whether a manager initiates or recommends a change is *courage*. Some managers like to "live dangerously" and would tend to initiate while others prefer to "play it safe" and recommend. In either case, they are taking a risk. If they recommend, the risk they are taking is that their boss will say *no*. And most managers would not only give up on that recommendation but would also hesitate to recommend other changes for fear they would be turned down. In the book *No-Nonsense Communication* (Kirkpatrick, 1983), it is suggested that managers not take no for an answer but follow the approach taken by a salesperson when a customer says no. First of all, the manager should learn how to handle objections. Secondly, if the boss says no, the manager should analyze the reason and try a different approach or pick a better time. It is said that on the average, a salesperson calls on a potential customer five times before making the first sale. Managers usually make a suggestion only once. If the boss says no, the subordinate usually forgets it and possibly refrains from offering future suggestions.

One risk that the manager takes in initiating instead of recommending is that the boss might be upset—even angry—because the manager didn't ask for approval. Another risk is that the idea is not a good one. The boss could have provided data to show why it wouldn't work. And serious consequences could result in terms of relationships and even job security.

In addition to recommending changes to the boss, managers also have opportunities to offer *recommendations to other departments*. To what extent they do it depends to a large extent on the rapport with other managers. If other managers are receptive, suggestions will be made. Managers will hesitate to recommend, however, if barriers exist such as hostility, jealousy, and negative attitudes (such as "You take care of your department and I'll take care of mine," or "Don't call me, I'll call you," or "If I want your advice, I'll ask for it").

Summary

The two key objectives of a manager are to contribute to the effectiveness of the organization and to get and maintain high morale. In order to do this, a manager should not only implement changes from above but also generate ideas for improvement. These ideas can come from many sources including subordinates, peers, and self.

The first role in managing change is to implement changes decided on by higher management. If the manager agrees that the change is good, he or she will be able to implement it enthusiastically. If, however, the manager feels that the change is for "worse" rather than "better," it is his or her responsibility to ask questions and even challenge the change. In the final analysis, the manager must implement the change or else seek another job.

The manager also plays a role of recommending changes. In making a recommendation to the boss, the manager should be sure the idea is a good one and then try to sell it. If the boss says no, the manager should carefully consider an alternative approach instead of giving up the idea. Managers should also play the role of recommending changes to managers in other departments. The ideas should be carefully considered first, and tact should be used.

Finally, a manager should play the role of initiating change, especially if the boss has given decision-making authority to the subordinate. Before deciding whether to initiate, a manager should carefully consider the significance of the change as well as its possible impact on other departments. If in doubt, it is safer to recommend and ask for approval.

3

ΟΙΟΙΟΙΟΙΟΙΟΙΟΙΟΙΟΙΟΙΟΙΟΙΟΙΟΙΟΙΟΙΟΙΟΙΟΙΟΙΟΙΟ

Philosophies, Principles, and Approaches from Authorities in the Field

In studying the literature relating to change, I analyzed many books. I looked for those that had practical application for managers in industry, business, and government. The following summary highlights the philosophy and recommendations from twelve sources. The rest of the chapter provides more details. In developing my model and recommendations for managing change, ideas of these authors were considered.

Philosophy and Principles

Bennett (1961, p. 3) emphasizes that "the attitude of the leader toward other persons is probably more critical than the change itself." This is important to remove feelings of insecurity that often accompany change. The leader needs to introduce support and help. Complete communication is needed to keep people fully informed about the objectives and procedures of the change. The process of change is helped when the persons who will be affected can participate in the decision-making process and in planning for the change. The most important task of the leader is to create the climate in which people feel that the leader has empathy for them.

A similar approach is described by Lippitt (1981). In planning for change, the manager must present the rationale for the change and provide opportunities for discussion. Those who will be affected must be involved in the decision-making process. Also, those who implement change must be sensitive to the concerns, anxieties, fears, hopes, wishes, and expectations of those who will be affected. Specific recommendations are made for brainstorming and a step-by-step process for implementing the change that has been decided on.

According to Odiorne (1981), people are more likely to change when they see some advantages in changing and some more disadvantages for not changing. Empathy on the part of managers is important to recognize these feelings. Participation and communication are important to make the decision to change as well as to get it accepted. The best option for change is one created by the people who must implement it or one for which the implementers can claim ownership.

Blake and Mouton (1982) emphasize that changes imposed on people sometimes succeed, but more often this approach fails. Resistance usually results from those expected to change their behavior. An alternative to the use of power and authority is to use the knowledge of norms to accomplish behavior change. This requires the involvement of those expected to change. It also requires an atmosphere that provides an opportunity for those affected to express their feelings and emotions. Chapter Fourteen is a case study in which the principles outlined by Blake and Mouton are applied.

Burack and Torda (1979) discuss rewards and punishment related to change. Rewards are effective if they relate to the value system of those affected. Penalties for not going along with a change may sometimes be effective. However, if genuine cooperation is the goal, it would be wiser to use other methods. The source of the change is an important consideration. Managers who have earned the respect of subordinates are more successful in getting their changes accepted than those who lack respect. Where managers participate with those at lower levels, the impact is even more positive.

Hersey and Blanchard (1972) describe four levels of change in people: knowledge, attitudes, behavior, and group changes. The list begins with knowledge, the easiest one, and proceeds to group changes, the most difficult. There are two ways to make changes. They can be called the "coerced" versus the "participative" change cycle. The coerced change cycle begins by imposing change. The participative change cycle begins by getting people involved. With mature groups, the participative style is usually more effective. With immature people, the coerced approach may be effective because they are often dependent and not willing to take new responsibilities unless forced to do so. The most effective approach is usually a blend of the two, depending on the situation.

Guiding Propositions

Margulies and Wallace (1973, pp. 154-157) describe six propositions that should guide an organization in managing change.

1. Any change effort in which changes in individual behavior are required, regardless of initial focus, must include means for ensuring that such changes will in fact occur.
2. Organizational change is more likely to be met with success when key management people initiate and support the change process.
3. Organizational change is best accomplished when persons likely to be affected by the change are brought into the process as soon as possible.
4. Successful change is not likely to occur following the single application of any technique.
5. Successful change programs must rely upon informed and motivated persons within the organization if the results are to be maintained.
6. No single technique or approach is optimal for all organizational problems, contexts, and objectives; diagnosis is essential.

According to Margulies and Wallace (1973, p. 157), "change is inevitable; it is a *natural process* and can be seen in the incessant flux of aging and evolution in all living systems. It need not, however, be seen as so troublesome, stressful, and indeed, catastrophic as some regard it. Change must rightfully be regarded as the vital, creative, exciting, and energizing force that it really is. Planned organizational change is one way that this magnificent energy can be harnessed for the good of persons everywhere."

Models

Some of the authors suggest a model or step-by-step approach that should be taken. Rogers (1962) states that an individual adopts a new idea or practice in a series of five steps:

1. First, the person becomes *aware* of the idea or practice, but doesn't know much about it.
2. Second, the person develops *interest* in the idea, looks for more information about it, and begins to consider its merits.
3. Third, the person begins to *evaluate* the idea, making mental applications to his own situation, and decides to try it.
4. Fourth, the person gives the idea a *trial*, usually on a small scale. Minimizing the risk at this stage is important, as is obtaining results for an adoption decision.
5. Fifth, if it has proven acceptable on a small scale, the idea is *adopted* for full-scale use.

Strategies for the effective management of change must consider these five steps as well as the social characteristics of the organization.

According to Schaller (1978), the process for managing change includes the following five steps:

1. *The self-identified discrepancy.* People discovering for themselves the discrepancy between current situation and the ideal.
2. *The initiating group.* Formation of the group to initiate the change.
3. *The supporting group.* Formation of a group to offer suggestions regarding the change and to support it.
4. *Implementation.* Putting the planned change into effect.

5. *Freezing the change*—institutionalizing the new set of conditions.

The challenge in implementing the fifth step is to prevent a slipping back to the former state of affairs but at the same time not fixing the change so rigidly that the current effort at freezing will be a barrier to further change in the future.

A very specific model was developed by Luthans (Luthans, Maciag, and Rosenkrantz, 1983) under the name Organizational Behavior Modification (O.B. Mod). This approach suggests the following steps to implement a change.

1. Identify the critical performance behavior.
2. Measure the behavior identified in step 1.
3. Analyze the behavior.
4. Intervene to accelerate the desirable performance behavior and decelerate the undesirable ones.
5. Evaluate the intervention to ensure that performance is indeed improving.

His model is based on observable behavior (not attitude or emotions) as the unit of analysis and the desired outcome as bottom-line results.

Buckley and Perkins (1984) outline a seven-stage model to identify the dynamics and impacts of transformative change.

1. Unconscious Stage. Recognizing the need for change.
2. Awakening Stage. Willing to move to the next stage.
3. Reordering Stage. Moving toward the change.
4. Translation Stage. Integrating information and visions of the first three stages.
5. Commitment Stage. Taking responsibility for the implementation of the change.
6. Embodiment Stage. Leaders and employees working together to implement the change.
7. Integration Stage. Developing a supportive environment of trust, cooperation, and openness.

Organizations that recognize these stages can plan and communicate effectively in order to manage change successfully.

Conner and Patterson (1981) have also developed a model. Theirs consists of three developmental phases including a total of eight stages.

Preparation Phase

1. Contact Stage. The earliest encounter a person has with the fact that change may take place or has already taken place.
2. Awareness Stage. The person knows that a change is being contemplated.

Acceptance Phase

3. Understanding Stage. The person demonstrates some degree of comprehension of the nature and intent of the change.
4. Positive Perception Stage. The person develops a positive view toward the change.

Commitment Phase

5. Installation Stage. The change is implemented and becomes operational.
6. Adoption Stage. The change has been used long enough to demonstrate worth and a visible positive impact.
7. Institutionalization Stage. The change has a long history of worth, durability, and continuity and has been formally incorporated into the routine operating procedures of the organization.
8. Internalization Stage. Persons are highly committed to change because it is congruent with their personal interests, goals, or value systems.

They emphasize that managers must be able to build commitment in order to manage change successfully.

Summary

Several common themes run through most of the writings. They can be summarized as follows:

1. Managers must understand the people who will be affected by the change. Their feelings and emotions will have much to do with the effectiveness of the change.

2. Change should not be forced on people. Otherwise, strong resistance will probably occur.

3. Effective communication is a must. People must be informed in advance and must understand the reasons for the change. Feedback for employees must be encouraged and listened to. If the ideas are used, credit must be given. If not, the manager should explain why the idea was not used.

4. People who will be affected by the change should be involved in the decision-making process.

5. It usually takes time for changes to be accepted. The more resistance, the longer the time. Therefore, planning should include the speed at which change is introduced.

6. Strategies for deciding on changes and getting them implemented must be developed. These strategies should be based on principles that will help to make the best decisions and get them accepted by those affected.

The following pages provide more details on the philosophies and recommendations of the writers that have been quoted. They are included in alphabetical order to make it easy for the reader to find those of particular interest. It should be noted that summaries of the writings of the authors may have omitted some key principles and approaches. Managers may want to go to the sources themselves, listed in the reference section, to read the selections in their entirety.

The Leader's Role in Managing Change
Thomas R. Bennett III

Some useful guides for managing change are:

- The attitude of a leader toward other persons is probably more critical than the nature of the change itself. *The more person-centered a leader is in his approach to a change effort, the more he is likely to be seen by others as friendly and supportive.*
- People fear change because it undermines their security. In introducing change of any kind, and of any magnitude, the leader needs to introduce support and help for the people affected.
- The process of change is helped when the persons who will be affected can participate in the decision-making process and in planning for the change. The leader needs to plan for ways in which persons can participate in the change process. The greater the participation, the more assurance people have of being able to influence the direction and impact of the change and, consequently, to identify and resolve their personal resistances.
- The leader should plan for both the emotional and the informational aspects of the change he is attempting. He needs to help people express their feelings about the change before and during the time it is being made. He needs also to keep people as fully informed about the objectives and procedures of the change as possible.

The following guidelines will help managers accomplish their change objectives:

1. *The leader needs to have ways of thinking about change.* This means that he needs some conceptual "models"—some reliable ideals that will guide his analysis of the situation in

Note: This selection is from *Planning for Change* by Thomas R. Bennett III, Leadership Resources, Washington, D.C., 1961.

which change is required and which will also serve to help formulate the process of change to be implemented.

2. *The leader must have clear goals.* In planning for a change, the leader must have a clear idea about the results which are being sought. Within his own thinking, this requires a resolute examination of the assumptions and the values which are being used to justify the introduction of the planned change. Some objectives or results will have a "must" quality to them—the change simply *must* be brought about or other crucial objectives cannot be attained.

3. *The leader should begin the change effort at the point where he has the most control and can make reliable predictions about the consequences of his actions.* For most of us, this point is within the day-by-day relationships in which we function. In these daily relationships with superiors, colleagues, and subordinates, a leader is likely to know more accurately what can be expected of other persons and what is expected of him. This is also the network of relationships in which he has the most self-control.

4. *The leader should recognize that change in any one part of the situation affects the whole.* What appears to be "a small change" actually can create a new environment in which people have to function. Many leaders recognize that "small changes" can create big problems unless the situation has been carefully analyzed to anticipate the consequences of each step in the change process. This means that any leader in planning for change must be alert for *unanticipated consequences* which cannot be preplanned but which must be dealt with in a flexible manner. This again emphasizes the importance of developing methods of participation for persons who are affected by the changes that are planned.

Managers can use the following questions as a change planning guide.

1. What is the difficulty that requires change in this situation? How did this difficulty begin? What is maintaining it?

2. What are my motives for attempting this change? What are the bases of my desire to promote this particular change?
3. What seems to be the present, or potential, reasons why others may support or resist the change?
4. What are my resources as a leader for giving the kind of help that seems to be needed now, or may develop as the change effort continues?
5. Have I made clear to those affected the purpose and extent of the change?
6. Have I made it possible for people to express objections openly?
7. To what extent can I involve in the planning those who will be affected by the change?
8. Once the change has begun, what do I need to do to stabilize and maintain it?

Some final points to keep in mind:

- The most important task of a leader is creating the climate that is conducive to the change being attempted. An emotional atmosphere in which people feel that the leader is empathic and nonjudgmental toward them and their needs is a climate in which persons will be more open about their feelings and resistances.
- In organizational and group situations, the development of orderly problem-solving processes will certainly help with the change. Such processes provide a maximum participation by those affected by the change. Consequently, it is imperative for the leader to plan methods and occasions through which people can participate in the change effort. This helps the change effort to become as self-motivated and voluntary as is possible in the situation.
- Persons affected by the change should have as much understanding about it and its consequences as is possible. To the extent that a leader will increase ways in which they can develop and control the direction of the change, to that degree he increases the trust which persons will have in his leadership.

- In any planned change the leader must give as much attention to the emotional dimension as is given to the informational aspects of the change effort. People cannot be persuaded out of their resistances and objections; however, they can be released from their fears when they are adequately informed and their feelings can be openly expressed and accepted. Change is truly accomplished when a new level of performance has been achieved without reducing the freedom of persons affected and without requiring constant pressure from a leader.

Establishing Acceptable Norms
Robert Blake and Jane S. Mouton

As a result of social blindness, managers who want to change behavior often disregard the existence of norms. Norms are the sinews that hold the corporate culture together. While cultures can't be seen and changed directly, it is possible to demonstrate the existence of norms.

A norm is any uniformity of attitude, opinion, feeling, or action shared by two or more people. Groups are characterized by the norms their members share. For all practical purposes, a group could not be a group if it lacked norms to regulate and coordinate interactions among members. The reason is that there would be no basis for coordination or cooperation. If norms were absent, we might refer to the individuals who are physically assembled in the same place as an *aggregate,* but not as a group.

The concept of norms and other concepts related to it (such as standards and traditions) are not often used to describe individuals. Groups have norms, but individuals usually are not pictured that way. We may speak of someone as having an attitude or attitudes, but it is more customary to speak of a group as having norms or traditions. Even though individuals are their "carriers," norms and traditions belong to groups, not individuals.

By contrast, concepts such as attitudes, opinions, and feelings convey something about individuals that groups may be said to lack. Individuals have opinions; groups do not. The same holds for attitudes and feelings. All these words describe something viewed from the perspective of the individual.

Bosses more frequently than not disregard or don't "see" norms and rely on the exercise of unilateral power to compel shifts in behavior even when these are resisted. A boss may say to a subordinate, "Shape up or ship out." This statement rests

Note: This selection is from *Productivity: The Human Side* by Robert Blake and Jane S. Mouton, Amacom, New York, 1982. Used by permission.

on the assumption that the command itself is strong enough to produce the desired behavior.

The strategy of changing behavior by "decree" is seen in the "a new boss sweeps clean" approach. A new boss takes over a job, sees things not to his or her liking, imposes his or her will on the situation, and tells people in a direct way to stop doing what they have been doing and to start doing what he or she wants done. The boss is using power and authority to break up prevailing norms. This method is sometimes successful, but far more often it fails. Those whose behavior is expected to shift resist. Though they themselves may not recognize that fact, they prefer to act in accordance with the prevailing norms that are held in place by the influence of colleagues rather than to follow a boss's directives. More often than not, they simply use passive resistance, although sometimes the resistance goes underground. Eventually the new boss comes to terms with it by recognizing his or her inability to introduce change at a rapid rate. Resistance to change has set in. Productivity remains at about the same level as before.

Relying on power and authority to change norms can be risky. Over and above the resistance it provokes, whether active or passive, there is the likelihood of alienating those who are expected to shift their behavior. These people may become resentful and even vengeful. Significantly lowered morale may make it even more difficult to realize the sought-after improvements.

Many bosses in a new assignment realize that their power and authority are weak, or perhaps they sense the adverse consequences that can arise from resistance to change. What do they do under these circumstances? Perhaps we might gain some understanding of the forces that operate by looking at another setting.

Commonly held norms and values make a group less susceptible to disruption from external forces. In an experiment with a group of children who had established ways of playing with toys, an older child who was a leader in another group was introduced as a new member of the group. The new child, in order to be effective, had to learn to act within the constraints of the new group, even though he was more of a leader than the other members. In order to be effective, the child had to learn the "rules" and then find ways to introduce his own modifications in order to exert influence on the other members of the group.

Managers in a new assignment may seek to exert influence but do little more to make their influence felt than change job titles or add a little bit of office decoration. The takeover is symbolic. Such a boss may wait several months until he or she has learned the ropes before trying to introduce real changes. The "go slow" boss learns the norms and standards that prevailed before attempting to introduce changes. However, the boss is more than likely to adopt the prevailing norms and standards. The result is that he or she becomes the spokesman for the normative culture of the group, and ultimately becomes part of it without exerting further influence on the group thereafter.

An alternative to exercising power and authority to command change is to use the knowledge we now have of norms and their influence on behavior to moderate behavior change. The way to change norms is to involve those whose behavior is regulated by them in studying what the existing norms are and exploring alternatives that might serve corporate objectives better. Only after prevailing norms are understood can specific steps necessary for shifting from the old to the new be considered and implemented. The key factor is to involve those who are controlled by a norm to change the norm itself. When the norm is shifted, altered attitudes and behavior consistent with the new attitudes can be expected to emerge. The following conditions are basic to success.

1. *All norms carriers actively participate.* Both primary and reference group members who are carriers of the prevailing norm must actively participate, because it is their support of new patterns of behavior or new norms of productivity (volume, quality, control of waste, and so on) that governs whether new approaches will prevail.

2. *Leadership is by those responsible for ultimate decisions.* There is no realistic prospect for changing norms and stan-

dards if those who are the leaders of the prevailing norm system absent themselves from the effort. The reason is obvious. If they do not think through the prevailing norms and the limitations in behavior that these create, they are in no position to give their leadership approval or the identification and development of new and more appropriate norms.

3. *Participants are involved with the problem.* Norms are likely to be anything but explicit and self-evident. Therefore, the problem is how to identify them so that they can be dealt with in an objective manner.

4. *Facts and data are provided about the objective situation.* Sometimes norms have been based on false information. When this is so, providing participants with objective evidence of the true state of affairs can facilitate the rejection of the old norm and the acceptance of one that squares better with the facts in the situation.

5. *Ventilation and catharsis are provided.* Those involved in a problem—both employees who practice the unproductive behavior and those who are responsible for it—are often frustrated by its continued existence. They blame others for it. Without the opportunity to get their frustrations and antagonisms into the open, they continue to find it difficult to think constructively about how the problem might be resolved. In these circumstances, it is essential to create an atmosphere that allows those who are a part of the problem to discharge their feelings and emotions. Only in this way is it possible to get the negative attitudes that are preventing constructive problem solving out of the way. Such emotions and feelings constitute evidence that members share a norm, one that they are likely to enforce on one another in a way that makes a deviant suspect.

6. *Reasons for the current problems are identified.* Participants often have different explanations of a problem. Discussion separates false from valid explanations.

7. *Implicit agreements are made explicit.* Whatever the discussions produce by way of proposed new attitudes and behaviors, the conclusions that are reached need to be crystal-

lized and validated by public agreement rather than simply presumed to be widely acceptable.

8. *Changes in norms are followed up.* New norms are always weaker than those they replace. The result is that people tend to backslide toward the norm that previously prevailed. Follow-up is essential to strengthen new attitudes and behavior and bring them into effective use.

Transformative Change
Karen W. Buckley and Dani Perkins

Transformative change is occurring in institutions and organizations around the world today. Caused by societal shifts as
dramatic as those which occurred in the Renaissance and during
the Industrial Age, the major premises and underlying patterns
of current society are being challenged. The challenge of the
80's is to maximize the great potential that exists during a transformative change for innovation, growth and positive development and minimize the confusion and turmoil inherent in the
disintegration and reformation of transformative change.

In an attempt to better grasp the dynamics of transformative change it is helpful to differentiate between transformation
and change. *Transformation* is a profound fundamental change
in thought and action which creates an irreversible discontinuity
in the experience of a system. *Change* is the modification of beliefs, behaviors and attitudes. Change is moving to another location on the same floor. Transformation is moving up a floor.
Leaders guiding a transformation find that in a transformation
multiple forces converge to catalyze the change.

Transformative change occurs on three levels: structure:
the patterns of the organization (i.e., reporting lines, job defini-
tions); behavior: the way the system acts (i.e., communication
patterns and relationships); and consciousness: the way things
are viewed (i.e., attitudes, beliefs and myths). The timing and
rhythm of the transformation is based on the entire system's
readiness to shift on each of these levels.

To move from the chaos of transformative change to peak
performance, it is necessary to understand the complex process
of transformation as it relates to organizational and individual
needs. The analysis and comprehension of organizational transformation is complicated by large numbers of people and other
factors in the environment. The various subsystems experience

Note: This selection is from *Managing the Complexity of Organizational Transformation* by Karen W. Buckley and Dani Perkins, edited by
John Adams, Miles River Press, Alexandria, Va., 1984. Used by permission.

change at different rates and affect each other in a converging pattern of cyclical waves. The individual employees, departments, divisions and subsidiaries are all involved in a dynamic interaction of different rhythms and tempos of change.

A seven-stage model is presented here that attempts to identify the dynamics and impacts of transformative change. A fully integrated transformative change requires movement through all seven stages of the cycle. The tempo and direction vary as the organization moves in a seemingly random manner, jumping backward and forward. Rhythm and timing are determined by the rate the change can be managed. Progression through the cycle can be instantaneous or ponderously slow. Often a micro-cycle of the seven stages is encompassed in each stage. The seven stages include: Unconsciousness, Awakening, Reordering, Translation, Commitment, Embodiment and Integration.

As organizations undergo major transformations necessary for survival and growth, individual employees' lives are also transformed. The success of an organizational change largely depends on the employees' ability to integrate the changes. The individual experiencing transformation in an organizational context will discover that a cycle of transformation begins in the Unconsciousness Stage.

1. *Unconsciousness Stage.* Organization transition begins gradually with a period of organization unconsciousness that builds a readiness for change. During this gestation, the organization develops the capacity to acknowledge that something is wrong. The clues that indicate that an organization is experiencing this stage include unconnected random information, sporadic symptoms and tentative new ideas. Recognizing the need for change, the organization enters the next stage of transformation.
2. *Awakening Stage.* The developing awareness and surfacing symptoms form a message to all involved of needed change. The message introduces instability into the system and disrupts the harmony of the previous plateau as it threatens

the status quo. The rate of awakening varies depending on internal and external conditions and the critical mass of people accepting the need for change and willing to move the organization into the next stage of reordering.

3. *Reordering Stage.* Reordering is a probing process integrating the new catalyst with the existing situation and beginning to challenge underlying assumptions of the past. The organization collects data to determine whether to make a minor change or embark on a more fundamental transformation. As the organization chooses a deeper level of transformative change, it must recognize that the magnitude of the impact is greater. The organization strengthens the transformation by early inclusion of those employees struggling to accept that what was no longer is. The organization begins to move toward the new vision that provides a sense of potential and benefit in the translation stage.

4. *Translation Stage.* Translation is the process of integrating information, metaphorical images and personal visions of the unconsciousness, awakening and reordering stages. The images evolve into a vision of what the organization wants to achieve, which then organizes and instructs toward the desired future. The cohesive, focused direction provides the foundation for a total commitment by the organization to the transformation in the next stage.

5. *Commitment Stage.* Commitment is when the organization takes responsibility for implementation of the new vision. The commitment stage is a pivotal point in the transformation cycle. So far, the organization and individuals have only been considering the possibility of transformation. This is the time when the level of ability and readiness "to travel the distance" become key factors. Resistance surfaces as individuals are torn between the potential of the new direction and the security of the old. If the individual is not prepared to handle these stresses, the transformation may revert to earlier stages, stagnate or die.

Based on an assessment of organization consciousness, attitudes and behaviors, it is important for leadership to decide whether to proceed with the next stage, embodiment, or to return to the previous stages for further development.

6.   *Embodiment Stage.* In embodiment, leadership and employees work together to bring the transformed vision into day-to-day operations. The challenge is to manage the interaction of three elements: (1) consciousness shifts: attitudes, beliefs and assumptions; (2) structural changes: patterns of organization; and (3) behavioral changes: actions, relationships, communications.

Embodiment is accomplished with experimentation, trial and error and a start/stop tempo without which embodiment results in short-term, superficial change. Eventually, the embodiment implementation is complete, and the organization and individuals reach a stage of integration where the consciousness, structural and behavioral alignment deepens.

7.   *Integration Stage.* As the embodiment of the desired change becomes widespread, the organization reaches a stage of integration. A supportive environment of trust, cooperation and openness is developed. The organization reaches a plateau of balanced wholeness and is experiencing peak performance as the informal and formal systems are aligned with the new vision of the organization. The integration stage is made up of varying degrees of completion. Through celebrations and rituals, the community is solidified and the disorientation and chaos transformation are healed.

The passage through the cycle is now complete, a stable foundation built and the organization once again enters the unconsciousness stage developing readiness for the next cycle of transformative change.

As we have seen, the process of transformation is essentially a death and rebirth process. In our traditional mechanistic bias, we have imagined that transformation comes through fixing something defective or supplying something that is missing. The seven stages characterize transformative change as a cyclical process of disintegration and reformation. Organizations and individuals use these stages to build a common language, to facilitate communication, to assess progress and to anticipate future needs. In the celebration of a transformative change the seven stages build a foundation for future change. Successful institutions are preparing for the complexities of change and transformation by building a state of readiness and planning ahead to manage the anticipated impacts of a major change. Business leaders today are challenged to meet the changing needs of the world while maintaining high levels of productivity.

Rewards and Punishment Related to Change
Elmer H. Burack and Florence Torda

Rewards and punishment are important considerations when changes are made. In organizational life, rewards may take material or nonmaterial form, ranging from simple recognition to elaborate testimonial dinners, and from prizes, salary increases, and bonuses to gaining a share of ownership. By definition, promotions are rewards—at least there is a face value.

Short of demotion, punishment in organizations may be more subtle in that the message must be read between the lines. Nevertheless there is no lack of techniques or descriptive vocabulary. People are "kicked upstairs," allowed to "cool their heels," transferred to "the sticks," and "passed over" in terms of promotion and raises.

Offhand, it would seem that rewards and punishment almost guarantee desired results, especially if the stakes are known in advance. The chances are certainly better if rewards are interpreted as appropriate or desirable to all concerned. How many of us really cared about gold stars for good spelling? Would candy bars have been more interesting? (Clearly, some dentists would have favored this reward.) Although it is true that some people go along with gold stars, especially if they feel this eventually leads to better things, others are not so eager or farsighted. If rewards are to work as true incentives to change, they deserve careful thought in relation to the value system of the target group. In addition, rewards should be possible to accept. A long and distant trip might be highly desirable but completely unrealistic as a reward for a person with young children.

With punishment, the picture is more complicated. You are probably familiar with the controversy as to whether it is possible to legislate compliance. Compliance may refer to equal

Note: This selection is from *The Manager's Guide to Change* by Elmer H. Burack and Florence Torda, Brace-Park Press, distributors, Lake Forest, Ill. Published initially by Lifetime Learning Division of Wadsworth Publishing, Belmont, Calif., 1979. Used by permission.

opportunity, environmental, or criminal issues. It is argued, first, that legislation creates a new reality that must (under threat of punishment) be responded to. Second, once there is acceptance of this (*how does change affect me?*)—the intended responses obtained—compliance tends to be accompanied by more basic change. If an employer strongly opposed to female employment is forced to hire women, for example, he may discover their value to his firm. This is another example of an environmental change.

The argument may be reversed. The compliant but opposed employer may sustain his beliefs about women (*do I want to change?*) by continuing to observe only what fits those beliefs or by treating women in such a manner that they cannot help but prove him right.

There is evidence to support both arguments. Laws or direct orders from the boss will usually produce outward compliance, even if in some cases there is only surface change. For example, a penalty for plant safety violations may be reasonably effective without changing actual attitudes toward safety. If genuine cooperation is the goal, it would be wiser to encourage change through additional or alternative methods.

Time sometimes runs out, however, and last-resort measures may be necessary to produce change. This was the case for a large chain of retail food stores that went to great lengths to prepare their managers for enlightened compliance with equal opportunity regulations. When it became clear that many managers were still failing to meet their new responsibilities, top management announced that salary increases and promotions were to be evaluated in terms of managers' support of the program. To further ensure change, it was stated that failure to comply would be grounds for dismissal.

But even forced change is not simply coercion if there are elements within a situation that are compatible with the new requirements. For instance, mandatory compliance with a new office procedure will meet with voluntary compliance if those who must follow the new system have the necessary skills to deal with it (*do I have the abilities to change?*) and if the system itself proves useful to them. For example, acceptance of computer-based systems is likely to be greater if affected employees can make sense of computer printouts.

Messages are most likely to be heeded when their source is powerful or respected. Those in an organization who have earned the esteem of others are also more likely to act as models for thought and behavior. Respected individuals can thus send very *personal* messages (*how does change affect me?*) This is an opportunity too often overlooked in organizational planning for change. Respect and admiration cannot be artificially manufactured—*earned* is indeed the right word in connection with such sentiments. It follows that individuals who have the respect of others should be sought out to pave the way for change or to ease people through the trauma accompanying change.

The ability to inspire special regard is operative throughout an organization. It cuts across formal authority. Friendship groups are an important source of direct or personal influence. As in the family, sustained day-to-day contact (in work groups, within departments, and so on) often creates common ties and a need for good standing within the group. As a result of shared activities, problems, and corresponding feelings of camaraderie and mutual dependence, such groups develop their own informal rules and goals. The messages their members send to each other may either complement or resist organizational objectives.

To describe this influence as pressure is not quite accurate. What takes place in cohesive groups is more fundamental and voluntary in nature. There is constant opportunity to exchange and assess views with respected co-workers. Trust allows people to let their hair down. A less defensive attitude means openness to change. Seen in this light, human relationships in a work context are a resource for bringing about change.

The role of management also deserves special comment. Either through default or choice, higher management is often invisible to large numbers of organization members. Sometimes a decision is made to avoid direct interaction with those at lower levels in the belief that this will better protect managerial objectivity and the freedom or creativity of subordinates. Whatever the reasons, management that is aloof, and therefore unknown, cannot exercise leadership or serve as inspiration (model for behavior) in the direct sense we have been discussing. Such management is at a disadvantage in promoting change and may even increase resistance to change owing to the tendency to regard the unfamiliar with suspicion. There is much to be gained when management personnel are not afraid to present themselves as real and at times vulnerable human beings. Where management moves beyond this to participate actively with those at lower levels in efforts connected with change, the impact is even more personal in its effects.

Obtaining Commitment to Change
Daryl R. Conner and Robert Patterson

Commitment is necessary for successful change implementation; yet most managers involved in organizational change activities know very little about what it is, what must be done to prepare for it, how it is developed and how it can be lost. In order to provide managers with a cognitive map of how commitment can be generated, the "Stages of Commitment to Organizational Change" model was developed. The model consists of three developmental phases (preparation, awareness, and commitment) with advancing stages in each phase. Each stage represents a critical juncture where commitment to the change can be threatened or facilitated.

Preparation Phase

Stage I: Contact. The earliest encounter a person has with the fact that change has or may take place.

For commitment to an organization change to be generated, participants must first pass through the contact stage. Regardless of the approach used, this first stage in the commitment process is meant to produce an awareness that a change has already taken place or may occur in the future.

Contact efforts, however, do not always generate the intended awareness. Change agents are often frustrated when, after repeated meetings and memos regarding an impending change, one or more targets are either not prepared for the transition or react with total surprise when the change actually occurs. For this reason, the commitment model separates contact efforts from actual awareness of the change. This distinction emphasizes the danger in assuming that the two are synonymous or that contact will automatically lead to awareness.

Stage II: Awareness. The person knows that a change is being contemplated.

Note: This selection is from *Building Commitment to Organizational Change* by Daryl R. Conner and Robert Patterson, O.D. Resources, Atlanta, Ga., 1981. Used by permission.

If the first stage is successful, the person in question is aware that modifications affecting his or her operation have occurred or are possible. Awareness of change, however, should not be interpreted as necessarily indicating a thorough understanding of the full impact of the change. In many cases, targets know that a change of some nature is imminent, but this awareness may be accompanied by confusion regarding specific ramifications. Targets may be unclear about the scope, nature, depth or even the basic rationale or intent of the change. Only if awareness develops into a general understanding of the change and its major implications will progress toward acceptance be achieved.

Acceptance Phase

Stage III: Understanding. The person demonstrates some degree of comprehension of the nature and intent of the change.

Once the contact effort has produced awareness and understanding, the person is, for the first time, in a position to make a judgment about the change. This judgment will be based on each individual's view of reality.

Once an interpretation of the available information has created an understanding of the change, the person has crossed the disposition threshold; here one begins to develop a tendency to think and act in certain ways toward the project. The person enters the acceptance phase by demonstrating a positive perception of the change. Resistance is evidence to the degree negative perceptions are expressed.

Stage IV: Positive Perception. The person develops a positive view and disposition toward the change.

Once a positive perception of the change has been developed, the person is faced with whether or not to attempt or to support implementation of the change. Perceiving a new procedure as positive is one thing; deciding to commit time, energy and other resources necessary to implement it is quite another matter.

If a positive perception of the change is developed, the person has reached a point of action, thus moving to the final phase of the process: commitment. Action at this stage means overtly supporting the decision to install the change.

Commitment Phase

Stage V: Installation. The change is implemented and becomes operational.

If the decision to install is acted on, a second milestone has been reached, the commitment threshold. Developing a predisposition toward a change is important, but achieving enough acceptance to build commitment to action is critical in successful change implementation. Stage V is the first opportunity for true committed action to be demonstrated. As stated earlier, commitment is characterized by investment of resources, consistency of action and subordination of unrelated short-term objectives to long-range goals. Once the decision to install a change has been reached and acted on, the commitment threshold has been crossed. The decision to install a change or use the new procedure is an important first sign of commitment, but does not represent the maximum support possible.

Stage VI: Adoption. The change has been used long enough to demonstrate worth and a visible positive impact.

After installation of the change and a successful early trial period, the adoption stage is reached. The adoption stage is similar in dynamics to the installation stage. Both stages serve as testing periods for the organization to assess the cost and benefits of the change. In both stages, those involved in the implementation effort face logistic, political and economic problems requiring continuing analysis and modification of the project. In both situations, the change is aborted if previously developed commitment is eroded because of unresolved problems.

Although the dynamics of installation and adoption coincide, the differences are important. Whereas installation is focused on initial entry problems, adoption is concerned with in-depth, long-term use problems. The installation stage is an early attempt to use the change, to see if it works and to identify the initial human and technical repercussions. The adoption stage is a testing period that focuses on the long-term implications of the change. During installation, the main question is

"Will this change work?" In the adoption stage, the question is, "Does this change fit who we are as an organization?" The shift is from "Can we do it?" to "Do we want to continue it?"

Although the level of organizational commitment necessary to reach Stage VI is impressive, a change project at this stage is clearly still in an evaluation period and can be terminated with relative ease. If after extensive use the change is successful, an advanced level of commitment is demonstrated by granting formal or institutional status.

Stage VII: Institutionalization. The change has a long history of worth, durability and continuity and has been formally incorporated into the routine operating procedures of the organization.

The length of time to move from installation through adoption to institutionalization will vary according to the organization and the nature of the change project, but usually a considerable amount of time is needed. During this transition period, the participants modify the change and adjust to its long-range impact and requirements. As the change matures, it becomes a natural part of the organization's culture or expected pattern of behavior.

When a change has been institutionalized, organization members no longer view it in a tentative manner. Those affected by the change are expected to use the new format as an integrated part of routine operations. The change is now the norm. The organizational structure is modified to accommodate the change, and rewards and punishments are designed to perpetuate its existance.

Institutionalization represents the highest degree of commitment to change that can be demonstrated by an organization; nevertheless, it presents some limitations and problems. If a change has been institutionalized, those affected by the change may be motivated to adhere to the new procedures, primarily in order to comply with the organizational imperative. The product of such an attitude is often that change implementation can be forced. But it occurs in such a halfhearted, inefficient manner that a full return on investment for the effort is minimized or at least diminished.

Stage VIII: Internalization. Organizational members are

highly committed to change because it is congruent with their personal interests, goals or value system.

For a change to achieve maximum support from participants, they must be driven by an internal motivation that reflects their own beliefs and wants as well as those of the organization. Whereas the organization legislates and imposes the institutionalization of the change, the participants control the internalization. When change has been internalized, participants engage in goal-oriented activities in order to satisfy their own needs, as well as those of the organization. This level of commitment goes much deeper than that at the institutionalized stage. At this last stage, people demonstrate ownership for the change by accepting personal responsibility for its success. Now the change is advocated, protected, developed and invested in to a personal degree no organizational mandate could ever generate.

Enthusiasm, high-energy investment, and persistence characterize commitment at the internalized level. This type of advocacy tends to become infectious, and often targets who have internalized a change cannot be distinguished from sponsors in their devotion to the task and their ability to engage others in the change effort.

Implications for Building Commitment to Change

The commitment model has many implications for those involved in designing and implementing significant changes within their organizations. The following are six of the most crucial lessons associated with commitment building in successful change efforts.

1. Commitment is expensive; do not order it if you cannot pay for it. Most sponsors want full support for changes they intend to implement, but lack understanding of the sophisticated dynamics required to develop it. When they do comprehend the investment of time, money and energy required they often balk at the expense.

A target fully committed to implementing an organizational change demonstrates a high degree of personal investment. To gain this kind of advocacy at the target level requires substantial individual and organizational investments by the sponsors and agents. For target commitment to develop they must be:

a. provided with information as accurate and complete as is feasible;
b. considered, and to the extent possible, involved in the planning and execution of the change project;
c. rewarded for their participation and assistance.

Requirements for target commitment are indeed expensive; yet the payoff, when the change is implemented successfully, is dramatic.

2. Commitment strategies must be developed. Typically, managers devote much time, money and energy to making the right decision regarding what should be changed and virtually no investment in building commitment to that decision. A well-thought out strategy will maximize the possibility that those involved will develop a high commitment toward successful implementation of the change. Strategies should not be limited to targets. Sponsors must develop plans to assure that their agents are fully supportive, and agents need to work at increasing the level of sponsor support.

Some change projects require only that people try the new format or procedure: *installation.* Other projects need a more extensive testing period: *adoption.* For many change projects, the intent of the effort will be lost unless the change becomes formally sanctioned: *institutionalization.* If the long-range goals of a change demand high levels of support, involvement, adjustment, and sacrifice from the participants, maximum commitment is necessary: *internalization.*

3. Building commitment is a developmental process. The events leading to commitment are sequential in nature: awareness, for example, is the result of successful contact; understanding must occur before a positive perception can be generated.

Obviously, sponsors can skip some steps by simply announcing that a change has already been institutionalized. When this approach occurs the announcement is made, behavior dictated, and compliance achieved. If the change has significant implications for the targets, the likelihood of commitment being generated is low. Forcing compliance assures the technical implementation of a change, but often sponsors neglect to calculate the long-range cost of recurring resistance.

Short cuts to high commitment do not exist. Each stage in the process depends on successful completion of prior stages. If internalization is desired, implementation plans and sponsor and agent behavior must be consistent with the sequential stages presented in the model.

4. Either build commitment or prepare for the consequences. The degree of commitment needed for successful organizational change is a function of two factors:

a.   the relative importance of the change project to the overall goals of the organization;
b.   the degree to which the change represents a disruption in the expectation patterns of participants.

The higher the importance and disruptive factors, the greater the need for increased commitment. Although building maximum commitment is important, at times logistic, political, or economic reasons make the cost for commitment too high. If full commitment is not feasible, preparation for the resulting resistance is necessary. Too often sponsors and/or agents decide not to invest in building target commitment, then they are surprised and unprepared for the inevitable resistance that occurs. Both sides of the fence cannot be played simultaneously.

5. Human reaction to change is a function of intellectual and emotional response cycles. People respond to change in predictable ways. Adjusting to an organizational shift requires that a person:

a.   observe that a change has occurred or is possible,
b.   develop an orientation toward the change by collecting information and establishing priorities,
c.   make a decision to support or resist the change, and
d.   take action on that decision.

The cycle begins again when the person is attentive to the impact that action has on the situation; thus one observes new changes occurring.

Response Cycle

Observation

Action   Orientation

Decision

The response cycle operates at two levels. It has an intellectual and an emotional component, each usually moving through the process at a radically different pace. The intellectual capacity most people have to observe, orient, decide, act, and observe again is dramatically greater than the capacity to move through the same sequence emotionally. The result is that participants in organizational change often achieve a level of intellectual commitment which far exceeds their emotional commitment. This split-level commitment can produce confusion, mixed signals, and ambiguous communications for all involved.

Managers of organizational change must learn to deal with both intellectual and emotional cycles of commitment, and implementation plans should account for the speed difference between the two. Managers must also learn to distinguish between deteriorating commitment and the mixed messages people produce when their heads have accepted the change, but their hearts are still struggling.

6. Recognize the power and responsibility of learning how to manage change. It is dangerous to attach blanket value judgments to change dynamics; i.e., commitment is always good, or resistance is always bad. Whether a particular change is good or bad, appropriate or inappropriate, valuable or destructive must be answered by participants from their own perspective.

This objective approach to the study of change allows one

to isolate and analyze the dynamics of commitment as a phenomenon regardless of value judgments which may be imposed in any one specific situation. Students of the change process must study its dynamics with objectivity, but this in no way implies neutrality toward the applications of these same dynamics.

Sponsors, agents and targets must recognize the power and corresponding responsibility which accompany learning the dynamics of commitment building. They must learn not only how to orchestrate certain variables to increase the likelihood of specific outcomes, they must also determine when to use these tools, whom and what they should support, and the long-range consequences of the change they implement.

Changes in People
Paul Hersey and Kenneth H. Blanchard

There are four levels of change in people:

1. Knowledge changes
2. Attitudinal changes
3. Behavior changes
4. Group or organizational performance changes

Changes in knowledge tend to be easiest to make; all one has to do is give a person a book or article to read, or have someone whom he respects tell him something new. Attitude structures differ from knowledge structures in that they are emotionally charged in a positive or negative way. The addition of emotion often makes attitudes more difficult to change than knowledge.

Changes in individual behavior seem to be significantly more difficult and time-consuming than either of the two previous levels. For example, a person may have knowledge about the potential dangers of smoking, even actually feel that smoking is a bad habit that he or she would like to change. Still, the person would be unable to stop smoking because a habit pattern has been reinforced over a long period of time. It is important to point out that we are talking about change in patterned behavior and not a single event. In our example, anyone can quit smoking for a short period of time; the real test comes months later to see if a new long-term pattern has evolved.

While individual behavior is difficult enough to change, when we get to the implementation of group or organizational performance, it is compounded because at this level we are concerned with changing customs, mores and traditions. Being a group, it tends to be a self-reinforcing unit and therefore a per-

Note: This selection is from "The Management of Change" by Paul Hersey and Kenneth H. Blanchard, *Journal of the American Society for Training and Development,* Washington, D.C., January 1972. Used by permission.

son's behavior as a member of a group is more difficult to modify without first changing the group norms.

The levels of change become very significant when we examine two different change cycles—the participative change cycle and the coerced change cycle.

A participative change cycle is implemented when new knowledge is made available to the individual or group. It is hoped that the group will accept the data and will develop a positive attitude and commitment in the direction of the desired change. At this level the strategy may be direct participation by the individual or group in helping to select or formalize the goals or new methods for obtaining the goals. This is group participation in problem solving. The next step is to attempt to translate this commitment into actual behavior. This tends to be the real tough barrier to overcome. For example, it is one thing to be concerned (attitude) about a social problem but another thing to be willing to actually get involved in doing something (behavior) about the problem. One strategy that is often useful is to attempt to identify informal as well as formal leaders within the group and concentrate on gaining their acceptance and behavior. Once this is accomplished you have moved a long way in getting others in the group to begin to pattern their behavior after those persons whom they respect and perceive in leadership roles.

We've all probably been faced with a situation similar to one in which there is an announcement on Monday morning that "as of today all members of this organization shall begin to operate in accordance with Form 10125." This is an example of a coerced change cycle. This cycle begins by imposing change on the total organization. This will tend to affect the interaction—influence the system at the individual level. The new contacts and modes of behavior create new knowledge which tends to develop predispositions toward or against the change. The intention of this coerced change cycle is that the new behavior creates the kind of knowledge which creates commitment to the change and therefore approximates a participative change cycle as it reinforces the individual and group behavior.

The participative change cycle tends to be more appropriate for working with mature groups since they tend to be achievement-motivated and have a degree of knowledge and experience that may be useful in developing new strategies for accomplishing goals. Once the change starts, mature people are much more capable of assuming responsibilities for implementation. On the other hand, with immature people the coerced change cycle might be more productive because they are often dependent and not willing to take new responsibilities unless forced to do so. In fact, by their very nature, these people might prefer direction and structure to being faced with decisions that might be frightening to them.

There are some other significant differences between these two change cycles. The participative change cycle tends to be effective when induced by leaders with personal power, while the coerced cycle necessitates significant position power—rewards, punishments, and sanctions.

With the participative cycle, the main advantage is that once accepted it tends to be long-lasting, since the people are highly committed to the change. Its disadvantage is that it tends to be slow and evolutionary. On the other hand, the advantage of the coerced cycle is speed. Using his position power, the leader can often impose change immediately. The disadvantage of this cycle is that it tends to be volatile. It can only be maintained as long as the leader has position power to make it stick. It often results in animosity, hostility and in some cases overt and covert behavior to undermine and overthrow.

These cycles have been described as if they were either/or positions. In reality, it is more a question of the proper blend of each, depending upon the situation.

Gaining Acceptance and Commitment to Planned Change
Ronald Lippitt

Any manager of a group that wants to achieve a meaningful level of acceptance and commitment to a planned change goal must present the rationale for the contemplated change as clearly as possible and provide opportunities for discussion to clarify implications and consequences for those who will be affected by the change. This is a necessary but usually not an adequate level of involvement to mobilize wholehearted collaboration and energy commitment to the change effort.

A chance for all those who would be involved to participate in an assessment of the way things are and the way things might be is a very important aspect of a humane process of change. With many groups and organizations we have started with what we call a "prouds" and "sorries" brainstorm of the way things are. The discussion and priority setting of the "proudest prouds" and the "sorriest sorries" does a great deal to create a climate of readiness to consider "how we would like things to be different." This is a very different process than the listing of gripes, which tends to generate negative feelings of frustration, depression, and scapegoating.

One of the most sensitive and energizing approaches to a planned change effort is the involvement of those who will be affected in projecting alternative images of potentiality for significant change. Often this involves the presentation for review of future scenarios beyond the experience of the participants. The provision of images of opportunity and possibility beyond what has been experienced is a very important responsibility and contribution of humane leadership, and usually involves drawing on technical resources from outside the group or organization.

Enthusiastic advocates of a change effort are often insensitive, and therefore inhumane, in avoiding a review and clarification of basic values that represent the carefully developed

Note: This selection is from *Making Organizations Humane and Productive* by Ronald Lippitt, Wiley, New York, 1981. Used by permission.

traditions and identities of the group. Usually change must and can build on respect for, rather than confrontation of, these basic aspects of group or organizational identity. They usually represent strengths to build on rather than impediments to progress. A careful consideration of "who we are" and "where we're coming from" is a crucial aspect of a humane process of change.

Every effort to initiate change, no matter how humane, activates an internal forcefield of ambivalence about maintenance of the way things are versus the risks and energies involved in a change effort. Insensitive change agents tend to ignore this underground of ambivalence or regard it negatively as "resistance to be coped with." The humane orientation toward the change process regards this ambivalence as a normal and necessary aspect of considering a commitment to a change effort, and provides opportunities for the open expression of the internal concerns, anxieties, fears, hopes, wishes, and expectations. From this open expression the change agent can derive much helpful information to assist in identifying blind alleys, potential traps, and important unexplored alternatives. In addition, the sharing of ambivalence provides the basis for clarifying issues and developing interpersonal support and objectivity. We have found that providing opportunities to articulate "internal dialogs" between the voices of caution about change and support for change is one of the most important aspects of supportive humaneness.

The quick death, halfhearted implementation, or subversion of many planned change efforts is the result of a separation of the goal setters, the planners, the implementers, and the constituents—those who will be served or affected by the change effort. Our psychological and sociopsychological research literature is full of evidence on the necessity of voluntary involvement in decision making if there is to be a wholehearted commitment to goals for action. Humane change agents have recognized that there are many levels and possibilities for involvement, ranging all the way from participation in information about the rationale and necessity for change to opportunity to be involved in initiating the needs for change and the goals for change. In all cases, significant involvement includes the invitation to be influential, and feedback that the input has been listened to and utilized. The consequences of neglecting such a process are disastrous to various degrees. At the best there will be halfhearted commitment and participation in the change effort, but more frequently there will be harmful consequences of neglect, irresponsibility, subversion, and alienation from the power structure.

In order to avoid depression and frustration related to change, the following steps should be followed:

1. What is the eventual outcome image you are moving toward? Be concrete in describing what it would look like if you were there.
2. Brainstorm with your team all the steps of action you can think of that might be steps toward the goal, including coping with the blocks you identified in your forcefield analysis.
3. Now review these possible steps and use what kind of sequence of steps there might be. Some things have to be accomplished before others, or two things need to be done at the same time. Create a possible "path of progress steps" visually for yourself.
4. Determine what seems to be desirable, even necessary, as a first step.
5. Determine who needs to be involved and how, in order to make the steps happen.
6. Determine how you will know when the first step has been achieved.
7. Determine how you will celebrate when the first step has been achieved.
8. Look for any evidence that things are off the beam or going too slow.
9. Determine whom you will replan with.

Organizational Behavior Modification
Fred Luthans, Walter S. Maciag, and Stuart A. Rosenkrantz

Much time, money, and effort is spent in training programs to change the behavior of supervisors and other managers. The desired results are improved productivity, reduced costs, and increased profitability. One successful approach is called organizational behavior modification (O.B. Mod). It has its roots in modern behaviorist psychology and, in particular, the work of B. F. Skinner. His principles of operant conditioning (that is, behavior is a function of its consequences) combined with the classic Law of Effect (behavior followed by positive consequences will tend to be strengthened and repeat itself; behavior followed by negative consequences will tend to be weakened and repeat itself less frequently) provide the basis for the prediction and control of employee behavior. The O.B. Mod approach assumes the following perspectives:

- *Observable behavior is the unit of analysis.* In an O.B. Mod approach, the focus is on critical performance behaviors that are observable and measurable. Thus employee attitudes, motives, or satisfaction are not of direct concern. Instead, the units of analysis are such behaviors as absenteeism, tardiness, and staying at the work station, or such "behavioral products" as the quantity and quality of work.
- *Emphasis is on systematic evaluation and "bottom-line" results.* In contrast to motivationally based approaches to human resources management (human relations training or job enrichment, for example), the O.B. Mod approach emphasizes the systematic evaluation of the intervention's impact on performance improvement. Irritating behaviors, such as complaints or unusual work habits, are not targeted for change unless an empirical relationship can be demonstrated between these behaviors and measurable, "bottom-line" per-

Note: This selection is taken from "O.B. Mod: Meeting the Productivity Challenge with Human Resources Management," *Personnel*, March-April, 1983, pp. 28-36. Used by permission.

formance. This emphasis on evaluation and performance allows O.B. Mod to meet the "accountability problem" facing all human resources management techniques today.

In addition to these two general perspectives, the steps by which O.B. Mod is implemented can be briefly summarized as follows:

1. *Identify the critical performance behavior.* This is probably the most important step because, like any problem-solving model, everything else flows from it. Such critical behavior must be observable and measurable and usually affects quantity and/or quality of performance.

2. *Measure the behavior identified in the first step.* The quantity and/or quality of output and the frequency of specified behaviors are usually available through existing records. Once these data are obtained, they are put into graphical terms (frequency over time). It is interesting to note that this measurement step itself may become an intervention (that is, cause the behavior to change because it is now being measured) and, if it does have the desired impact on performance, this is fine. However, the intent of the O.B. Mod process at this step is simply to determine how often the critical performance behavior is really occurring under existing conditions. When put to the test of measurement, the results (both good and bad) are often quite surprising.

3. *Analyze the behavior.* A functional analysis of the antecedents that cue the behavior or set the occasion for the behavior to occur and of the consequences that currently maintain the behavior is carried out in this third step of O.B. Mod. This A-B-C (antecedent-behavior-consequence) analysis provides important information for developing an effective intervention strategy. In some cases the critical behavior is not occurring because, on the antecedent side, the employee does not know what the goals are or does not have the proper training or equipment/information to behave properly. In most cases, however, the problem stems from the consequence side. Although the antecedents serve as a cue to trigger the behavior and therefore can control it, the behavior is still a function of its conse-

quences. Thus the intervention strategies are concerned mainly with the behavior's consequences.

4. *Intervene to accelerate the desirable performance behaviors and decelerate the undesirable ones.* The major intervention strategy is to provide both feedback on the critical performance-related behavior and positive reinforcement for progress and attainment. The more immediate, objective, accurate, and positive this feedback is, the more effective it becomes as an intervention for improving performance. The accompanying positive reinforcement can take many forms. Most often, simple attention ("They know that you know.") and recognition are more effective and longer lasting than "sugar-coated" praise. The key is that this reinforcement must be administered only when performance improves. Most pay plans do not meet the criteria of this type of contingent administration and thus they are not an effective reinforcement strategy for day-to-day performance behaviors. However, feedback/attention intervention strategy that is recommended under the O.B. Mod approach is not only contingent on performance but really costs the organization nothing.

5. *Evaluate the intervention to ensure that performance is indeed improving.* This evaluation utilizes that data that were initially gathered in step two and tries to be as sophisticated as possible.

Guides for Managing Change
Newton Margulies and John Wallace

For the manager concerned with the problems and issues of organizational change, there are many specific interventions that are available. Depending upon the constraints and requirements of the particular situation, the manager can choose among a wide variety of available methods and techniques. Implicit, however, in any approach or strategy for change are several guiding propositions about change and the change process. These propositions have some empirical basis and are also in some ways a conglomeration of values about change processes. Perhaps more importantly, they represent potentially testable hypotheses about change.

Proposition 1. *Any change effort in which changes in individual behavior are required, regardless of initial focus, must include means for ensuring that such changes will in fact occur.*

This rather obvious proposition is consistently ignored by both practitioners and theorists of organizational change. Academics continually debate the relative worths of "structure versus people," "technology versus structure," "technology versus people," "people versus structure," etc., as the basic target of change. The socio-technical movement has done little to resolve the debate. Such polarization is unfortunate. It fails to grasp the reality of the systemic properties of complex contemporary organizations. Discussions of dichotomies in organizational change are, or should be, a part of our past and we should move on to more fruitful discussions of systemic features. From this perspective, changes in organizations can (and do) begin anywhere —in management structure, in technology, or in people. In the final analysis, however, changes in the *behavior of the individuals who cause the organization to function* must occur. These necessary changes cannot be left to chance. Indeed, they must be planned for with careful concern for implementation and reinforcement.

Note: This selection is from *Organization Change: Techniques and Application* by Newton Margulies and John Wallace, Scott, Foresman, Glenview, Ill., 1973. Used by permission.

While it is true that changes in structure or technology must be accompanied by planned "people" changes, we must not overlook the converse of this statement. Changes in an organization's human systems may also give rise to the necessity for planned changes in management structure, and even, perhaps, in technology and other aspects of the task environment. For example, as values reflecting greater participation and openness develop, management structures and processes characterized by extreme position authority and secrecy may have to adapt. And while it is perhaps difficult to imagine how changes in persons might affect organizational technology, it is not impossible. We live in an age of intense alteration of human values. It is entirely conceivable that demands will be made both from within and from without to alter technological processes, especially those that continue to affect the human ecosystem and the general quality of working life.

Proposition 2. *Organizational change is more likely to be met with success when key management people initiate and support the change process.*

Planned change efforts must have the support and understanding of important management personnel if they are to proceed smoothly and produce desired effects. While there are undoubtedly exceptions to this rule, it is generally true that planned change efforts without support from top management and other persons in positions of leverage are at a great disadvantage. The point is that there is no substitute for an informed and sophisticated management that acts collaboratively in planning and implementing change.

Proposition 3. *Organizational change is best accomplished when persons likely to be affected by the change are brought into the process as soon as possible.*

Change is a threatening and anxiety-producing prospect to many people. While there are, of course, numerous exemplary people who can adapt to nearly anything, the vast majority of us are merely human. Nobody appreciates the *fait accompli* except the person who manages to pull it off. For the most part, sudden and unexpected change creates and intensifies *resistance* to change. Involving people early in the change process not only acclimates them to the idea of change but permits them to take a hand in those changes which are likely to affect their jobs, relationships, and personal satisfactions.

Proposition 4. *Successful change is not likely to occur following the single application of any technique.*

Changes in behavior require time, nurturance and effort if they are to be incorporated as stabilized patterns of action. Meaningful and "real" change is a long-term endeavor. Most organization change may be more cosmetic than substantive. Moreover, change of this sort is fragile requiring repeated reinforcement.

Proposition 5. *Successful change programs must rely upon informed and motivated persons within the organization if the results are to be maintained.*

External consultants are often useful to an organization in the preliminary stages of diagnosis, designing the program, and implementing the initial efforts. Such resource persons, however, cannot be counted upon to sustain the organization's efforts over time. The business of the maintenance of change must fall to resource people *within* the organization. Such valuable internal resources do not develop by chance. These persons must be trained, developed, and given the same managerial legitimacy as other respected and valued members of the organization.

Proposition 6. *No single technique or approach is optimal for all organizational problems, contexts, and objectives; diagnosis is essential.*

There are no magic panaceas in the organizational change technique repertoire, and "shotgun therapy" (random application of a single presumably potent technique or of a combination of them) should most certainly be avoided. The problem, as we have tried to make clear, is a management *decision* problem. One must match the approach to the need, the situation, the constraints, and the objectives.

Since the application of change techniques requires *informed managerial choice,* it is very clear that the effectiveness of any approach depends upon the quality of diagnosis that precedes its selection. As in any managerial decision, faulty and incomplete prior analysis will result in poor decisions and ultimately in an ineffective change project.

One final statement is in order. This concerns *means* versus *ends* in the application of the techniques we have described. Techniques such as team development, intergroup exercises, and laboratory training are *not* ends in and of themselves. They *are* means (tools) to reach clearly defined organizational change goals. It sometimes happens that managers, consultants, and organization members become so enamored with the intriguing world of personal development and interpersonal interaction represented in the techniques of change that they forget their original purposes.

This discussion of some important propositions concerning change recognizes the forces, both within and without the modern organization, that call for a management sophisticated (informed consumer) in the most recent developments in implementing such changes.

Change is inevitable; it is a *natural process* and can be seen in the incessant flux of aging and evolution in all living systems. It need not, however, be seen as so troublesome, stressful, and, indeed, catastrophic as some regard it. Change must rightfully be regarded as the vital, creative, exciting, and energizing force that it really is. Planned organizational change is one way that this magnificent energy can be harnessed for the good of persons everywhere.

A System for Managing Change
George Odiorne

It is apparent that the most likely tendency of normal people is to be *noncommitters*. This tendency will become more prevalent as life becomes more complex, as people become more educated, and as professionalism ensnarls more and more of our lives. A system for managing change means that we will produce change, but we won't do it by cramming it down the throats of people who are firmly attached to activity as it is being carried on now. Rather, the system of producing change must meet these requirements:

1. Management faces the fact that specialization produces the activity trap, and people will tend toward being noncommittal in decisions that might produce changes in their behavior.
2. Management needs to turn people from noncommitters into *reasonable* adventurers, to use a term coined by Roy Heath. This means the people cannot be expected to be plungers or blind risk takers, but that given a procedure acceptable to them and their professional cast of mind, they will make decisions that produce changes in an orderly fashion.
3. The key to turning noncommitters into reasonable adventurers while avoiding wild plunges into a murky or concealed future lies in getting people to see the reasonableness and professionalism in *widening their options* when confronted with a decision.

People are more likely to change when they can see some advantages in changing and some more disadvantages in not changing. The presentation of a wider range of options can change decision making. The first step is to *specify the problem in explicit terms as a deviation from a standard*.

Note: This selection is from *The Change Resisters* by George Odiorne, Prentice-Hall, Englewood Cliffs, N.J., 1981. Used by permission of the author.

The problem needs to be stated as the difference between what is and what should be. You have now turned the problem into an objective. At this point we are now ready to start seeking some options. Four rules will make options work:

1. *Take enough time to explain the problem.* This usually means involving as many people as necessary to get all of the available opinions and options.
2. *Build acceptance into the process early.* As Norman R. F. Maier points out, the final decision must have attributes of both quality and acceptance.
3. *Take enough time to hear the details of every option.* For many people at work, the major question to be asked of the boss is *What do you really want?* Once that has been spelled out, they are willing to go along and cooperate.
4. *Take enough time to arrive at a consensus.* If the boss or leader takes the time to listen to all views before deciding, he or she may find that consensus can be shaped.

The function of the decision maker should be to press for more options, until the best emerges. Options can be one of the following types or a combination:

Option 1. Do nothing different. Doing nothing different is a perfectly sound defensive option that should be explored before all others. If after a waiting period the problem will resolve itself, then it is pointless to spend a lot of time and money to jiggle with it.

Option 2. Find (and fire) a scapegoat. One of the common defensive options in the time of a change that threatens an organization is to try to find someone *who is wrong* to fire or displace.

Option 3. Reorganize the company. A major reorganization of the company or department is a defensive option.

The three options outlined so far, which of course also permit numerous variations, are not proposed as action plans to be adopted universally but as options which should be considered and either accepted or consciously rejected in every major decision. They are, of course, all defensive options. They prevent losses. They keep us or our organizations from sliding backward. They are often related to problems and threats that surround us.

Option 4. Define something noble about a proposed change. There are numerous ways you can define noble options that place you in an initiating posture rather than a defensive stance.

Option 5. Being creative and self-actualizing. Perhaps the best option for managing change is to propose that people move up to the highest level of human potentiality, that of prompting others and ourselves to live at a level of our highest potentialities.

Here are some of the specific things that we as parent, boss, or teacher can do to elicit the innovative and creative behavior to produce orderly and satisfying change.

- We can state explicitly that we desire to see such creative behavior.
- We can ask for commitments to innovation and change.
- We can arrange our systems in such a way that rewards and reinforcements flow to people who are self-actualizing and are denied to those who are stifling their own and others' best qualities.
- We can inform people when we observe that they are moving toward exemplary behavior, and reinforce it by our praise.
- We can demand that effort at less than one's best level be redone at a higher level. This higher level is that of the exemplary performer, or the highest potential of the person as he or she now stands.
- We can use the skills of interrogation to help people find where their highest potential might be.
- We can remove the obstacles that bar people from fulfilling their potential for growth and change.
- We can use the tools of recognition and achievement motivation to make exemplars of those who are fulfilling their highest potentials.
- We can speak the language of success rather than the sour words of failure.
- We can organize people into groups to reinforce one another on their path.
- We can leave people alone while they are working on their

goals and give them freedom to fail or succeed, and to reward and punish themselves.

The emphasis has been upon a key means of introducing change in a world of change resisters. The bureaucrat, the professional, the conservative, and the traditionalist all fuel the anti-change, anti-planning behavior of society. Exhorting such people is useless, and ordering them autocratically will merely produce resistance, for without their acceptance, no change will be implemented even when it is directed.

Lincoln once said that a mind stretched by a new idea never returns to its original dimension. Herein lies much of the power of the option. It is a possible route for introducing a new idea, teasing and eliciting it from the mind of its maker. This causes the idea to originate in the person who must implement it, which is perhaps the only way in the world of professionals for such change resistance to be overcome. Methods of aggressive selling or authoritarian directives to produce change will merely stiffen the level of resistance.

The best option for change is one created by the people who must implement it, or one for which the implementers can claim ownership.

Steps in Adopting Change
Everett M. Rogers

An individual adopts a new idea or practice in a series of five steps:

1. *Awareness.* The individual learns of the existence of the idea or practice, but has little knowledge of it.
2. *Interest.* He develops interest in the idea, seeks more information, and considers its merits.
3. *Evaluation.* He makes mental application of the idea, weighs its merits for his own situation, and decides to try it.
4. *Trial.* He tries out the idea, usually on a small scale. He's interested in minimizing risk at this stage as well as evaluating the results of the trial for an adoption decision.
5. *Adoption.* If the idea proves acceptable on a small scale, it's adopted for full-scale use.

The diffusion process takes place within a setting of a social system; that is, a community, an organization, or a voluntary group. The social system has a marked effect on the behavior of the individual. Ignoring this effect often leads to developing programs that urge the individual to change without considering the situation in which he lives and the effect of that situation on the new behavior he's being pressed to adopt.

Therefore, it's essential that a thorough analysis be made of *both* the individual and the social system. Security, anxiety, personal values, social status, norms on innovativeness, mental abilities, and conceptual skills are individual characteristics that should be analyzed.

Social system characteristics include norms on innovativeness, economic constraints and incentives, social constraints and rewards, and task characteristics of a group. The purpose of the analysis is to develop a complete diagnosis of the situation to help determine appropriate program development strategies.

Note: This selection is from *Diffusion of Innovations* by Everett M. Rogers, Free Press, New York, 1962. Used by permission.

A Process for Managing Change
Lyle Schaller

The process for managing change includes the following five steps:

1. *The Self-Identified Discrepancy.* One way of looking at the concept of the self-identified discrepancy is to contrast it with a very common approach to change in which an "outsider" identifies for members of a group the discrepancy between their current situation and the ideal. While this is not a completely useless approach, it is far less effective than enabling people to discover the discrepancy for themselves. This includes enabling others to both define the ideal and to discover the difference between that ideal and their current situation. For the change agent, this concept is one of a half-dozen most valuable tools as he/she goes about the business of initiating and facilitating the process of planned change.

2. *The Initiating Group.* The second phase of the process of planned change is the formation of the initiating group. There is a vast difference between sitting around complaining about the current situation and actually beginning to do something about it. This is the difference between the first and second steps in the process of planned change. It is also the first point at which the process may break down. The number of persons who find it easy to complain about contemporary conditions is far greater than the number who are willing to share in efforts to introduce change. One result of this is that the agent of change often finds it easier—and frequently more enjoyable— to work at increasing the degree of discontent than to organize the necessary initiating group.

3. *The Supporting Group.* There are six essential elements that are present in an effective supporting group. The first is numbers. The second essential element of an effective supporting group is the capability to legitimatize a proposed change. This "stamp of approval" often is essential to gain certain other

Note: This selection is from *The Change Agent* by Lyle Schaller, Abingdon Press, Nashville, Tenn., 1978. Used by permission.

required support. A third essential element in the building of a supporting group is loyalty. The importance of loyalty is sometimes overlooked in the efforts to develop a supporting group. The fourth essential ingredient in an effective supporting group is skill or expertise, and especially the combination of dedication and skill. This skilled leadership is necessary first to gain the necessary approval or adoption of the proposed change and, second, to make the change an operational reality. A fifth element that often is an essential element of an effective supporting group is expressed in the concept of a coalition. This is a substantially different concept than the one reflected in sheer numbers. Whether for better or for worse, the decision-making process in American society in this century has been dominated by interest groups and coalitions of interest groups. This leads into the sixth, and what may be the most essential, element in an effective supporting group. This is the capability of the members of the supporting group to take an idea or a proposal for change that is a response to discontent and that has been developed by the smaller initiating group and to revise or modify it and to adopt it as "ours!" This almost invariably means some compromises between the proposal for change developed by members of the original initiating group and the suggestions emerging from persons or factions that constitute the larger supporting group. The complexity of this is intensified when the time dimension is recognized. This means that as the supporting group grows with the passage of time, and as new persons or groups join this alliance, the proposal for change is being reworked and revised, compromises are being arrived at, and a growing number of individuals and groups feel a personal identification with the proposal for change. One of the most remarkable dimensions of this process is that as the proposal which originated back in the smaller initiating group is subjected to amendment, revision, compromise, and alternation, it is improved in quality. For the change agent this means he should not only look at this concept of a supporting group for political reasons but also as a means of improving the quality of the proposals for change and for developing a process of planned change which is of a continuing nature. This is a sharp contrast to the traditional view of change as a series of isolated and distinct episodes each separate from another in both time and process.

4. *Implementation.* In a great many efforts at planned change, this fourth phase in the process is a mere formality. If all of the homework has been done in the first three steps, this fourth step of implementation may appear to be both unexciting and easy. In most efforts at implementing change, four resources are necessary. The first is a skill in the implementation of ideas. A second resource is personnel. A third essential resource is goodwill. The fourth resource that is essential to the implementation stage is loyalty.

5. *Freezing the Change.* The final step in the process of planned social change is to institutionalize or freeze the new set of conditions. This can be accomplished by a variety of methods. It is possible to take certain irreversible steps and thus freeze the new change. In looking at the basic issue of institutionalizing change at the new equilibrium, the agent of change may find it helpful to ask himself three questions:

- Is it necessary, or even desirable to freeze or to make permanent this new set of conditions? Frequently the answer will be in the negative.
- How can the advocates of change freeze the changed set of circumstances? While the answer to that question varies with the circumstances, the same four points keep reappearing: Increasingly, legislation, the law, and the courts are involved in institutionalizing change; the resources (skill, personnel, goodwill, and loyalty) necessary for implementation tend to be the same resources required for freezing the change; persistence is the name of the game throughout the process of planned change, from enlarging the degree of discontent to freezing the new point of equilibrium; and the larger or the more firmly the organization is bound up in tradition, the more difficult it is to institutionalize a change unless the values, direction, and orientation of the organization are changed.
- How can the change be stabilized at this point of equilib-

rium to prevent a slipping back to the former state of affairs, but not fixed so rigidly that the current effort at freezing will be a barrier to further change in the future? There is no easy answer to this question.

CI

Why People Resist
or Welcome Change

It used to be an accepted fact that everyone resists change. We now know that it is not true. There are many reasons why a person resents (negative attitude) and/or resists (active opposition to) a particular change. Likewise, there are many reasons why a person accepts (neutral attitude) and/or welcomes (positive attitude) a particular change.

Why People Resent or Resist Change

There are many reasons why employees may react negatively to change.

Personal Loss. People are afraid they will lose something. They might be right or they might be wrong in their fear. Some of the things they might lose are as follows:

- *Security.* They might lose their jobs through a reduction in force or elimination of their jobs. Automation and a decline in sales often bring about this feeling.
- *Money.* They might lose money through a reduction in salary, pay, benefits, or overtime. Or, expenses such as travel may be increased because of a move to another location that is farther from their home.
- *Pride and satisfaction.* They might end up with jobs that no longer require their abilities and skills (that is, a "button

pusher" instead of a "skilled craftsman"). Automation such as computer-aided design (CAD) in engineering departments often results in this type of loss.

- *Friends and important contact.* They might be moved to another location where they will no longer have contact with friends and important people. This loss of visibility and daily contacts is very serious for people who are ambitious as well as those with a strong need for love and acceptance. In Puerto Rico, for example, families who had lived in slum conditions didn't want to move into low-cost multiple-story housing built by the government.
- *Freedom.* They might be put on a job under a boss who no longer gives them freedom to do it "their way." Closer supervision that provides less opportunity for decision making is a dramatic loss to some people.
- *Responsibility.* Their jobs might be reduced to menial tasks without responsibility. This may occur when a new boss takes over or through changes in methods or equipment.
- *Authority.* They might lose their position of power and authority over other people. This frequently happens when reorganization takes place or when a new boss decides to usurp some of the authority that an individual had.
- *Good working conditions.* They might be moved from a large private office to a small one or to a desk in a work area with only a partition between people.
- *Status.* Their job title, responsibility, or authority might be reduced from an important one to a lesser one with loss of status and recognition from others. This also happens when another layer of management is inserted between a subordinate and manager.

No Need. The typical reaction is, "What's the matter with the way things are now?" Or, "I don't see any reason why we should change."

More Harm Than Good. This is even stronger than the previously mentioned "No Need." People really feel it is a mistake —that it will cause more problems than it's worth. And sometimes this reaction is justified. It is particularly common when people at the "bottom" of an organization feel that top management makes changes without knowing what's going on "down on the line."

Lack of Respect. When people have a lack of respect and/ or negative attitude toward the person responsible for making the change, there is a strong tendency to resent and even resist it. Their feelings don't allow them to look at the change objectively. This would apply to attitudes toward a particular person as well as toward the department the person represents. For example, production foremen may not respect the industrial engineering department or anyone who represents it.

Objectionable Manner. Sometimes change is ordered in such a way that the people resent and/or resist because they don't like being told what to do. The emphatic command "Do it!" and/or a derogatory tone can create emotions that would not have resulted if the persons had been asked to do it in a nice way. This feeling can also occur if people are told what to do but not told why.

Negative Attitude. People with a negative attitude toward the organization, the job, and/or the boss are very apt to resent or resist change no matter what it is. This is one of the reasons why high morale is so important.

No Input. One of the most significant reasons is the fact that the people who felt they should have been asked were not asked for their ideas concerning the change. This will be discussed in detail in Chapter Eight.

Personal Criticism. Whether or not the change is actually criticizing the things that were previously done or the way in which they were done, people may look upon the change as a personal criticism. For example, a person who has developed a certain system or procedure will very likely take it personally if someone wants to change it. Resentment and possible resistance can result.

Creates Burdens. Some changes add more work and with it confusion, mistakes, and other negative results. The computer, for example, has been forced on many departments, and burdens and additional problems result. People, therefore, will naturally resent and even resist such a change.

Requires Effort. The change will obviously require more effort. And much of the effort accomplishes very little, if anything. Whenever changes require more time and effort, people are apt to resent and even resist them, particularly if no rewards accompany the extra effort.

Bad Timing. The timing of a change is very important to its acceptance. If it comes at a time when people are already having problems, the change is usually resented and probably resisted by those who are supposed to implement it. If, for example, a subordinate is in the process of making a schedule change that had been ordered by the boss, the subordinate would resent and probably resist another schedule change that the boss might request or order.

Challenge to Authority. Some people are testing their power and influence by simply refusing to do it. A typical comment might be, "I won't do it and there is nothing you can do about it!" It is usually done to see whether or not the subordinate can get away with it.

Secondhand Information. Some people are very sensitive about the way they learned of the change. If they found out about it from a secondhand source, they might resist it until they hear it "from the horse's mouth."

What Is the Real Reason for Resentment or Resistance? Managers often have difficulty in determining the real reason why subordinates resent and/or resist a change. They may feel that the subordinates are just being stubborn or that they are afraid they will lose something. The real reason may be entirely different.

A personal example will illustrate how manager and employees may view resentment and resistance differently. When I worked for International Minerals and Chemical Corporation (IMC), I got a new boss named John. I had worked for IMC for twenty months and had developed and installed a new performance appraisal program. After being there for about two months, my new boss called me into his office. The conversation went something like this:

John: I was talking with some of the executives of our accounting department and they are interested in a performance appraisal program.

Don: Good.

John: I've looked over the manual that describes the performance appraisal program that you've developed and implemented here at IMC. After studying it carefully, I've determined it's too complicated for the accounting department. They want a simple program that will be easy to install and maintain.

Don: I'm sure that I can talk with them and explain the benefits of my program so they will accept it.

John: I've decided that it needs to be simplified into a one-page form that will be easy to fill out by the manager.

Don: I don't feel that that kind of approach will be effective.

John: I've set up a dinner meeting with them in about a month and I promised that we'd present a simplified approach that will be tailored to their situation.

Don: I know your feelings, John, but I'm convinced that the program I have developed will be of much more benefit. And I'll help them train their managers so it won't be that difficult to implement.

John: I already told them we'd come up with a simple approach and I want you to modify the program and present it to them at that dinner meeting.

Don: Have you talked to anyone at IMC where I've installed the program?

John: No, I don't have to. I've studied your manual and I know just what you did.

Don: I suggest that you talk with Jack Devlin at Carlsbad or Bill Ramsay at San Jose or Bob White at Bartow. I've installed the program at all three of their locations and their accounting people are using the program.

John: I don't need to talk to them. I've already made up my mind and told them we'd simplify the program and reduce the forms to one page.

Don: If you are so convinced that a simple one-page form is the answer, then you make the presentation because I'm not going to do it!

John: (After a pause) I'll talk to you later.

At this point, I left John's office wondering what would happen. John would probably have liked to fire me or at least

take some disciplinary action but he felt that it would be un-
wise because of the short time he had been there. So he went to
his boss, Austin, and the conversation went something like this:

Austin: What's on your mind, John?
John: I just talked to Don about working with the account-
           ing department on a new performance appraisal pro-
           gram.
Austin: What happened?
John: Don said he wouldn't do it. He told me that I should
           do it myself if I felt so strongly that it should be a
           simplified approach.
Austin: Don actually told you he wouldn't do it and you
           should do it yourself?
John: Yes.
Austin: I wonder why he said that?

Here are the reasons that John gave to Austin:

- Loss of pride in being forced to modify the program.
- Resentment toward me. He probably didn't like the fact that
  I was hired from the outside to be his boss.
- Personal criticism. He probably took it personally that I crit-
  icized the program he developed.
- Required effort. He would have to spend time and energy to
  modify his approach.
- Challenge to authority. Because of his seniority, he maybe
  tried to see how far he could go in resisting my supervision.

Austin called me into his office and the following conversation took place:

Austin: Is it true?
Don: Is what true?
Austin: Is it true that you told John that you wouldn't pre-
           sent a simplified performance review program to our
           accounting department?

Don: Yes, it's true. I told him that if he was so convinced that a one-page form was the answer, he should do it himself.

Austin: Why did you tell him that?

Don: It is very simple. What he asked me to do would be a mistake. I considered the simplified one-page approach when I developed the program. It just won't do the job in building relationships and helping subordinates to improve their performance. By the way, did John tell you that he hasn't talked with anyone at IMC in order to evaluate the effectiveness of the program I've developed?

Austin: No, he didn't tell me that.

Don: I didn't think so. I told him to talk with Jack Devlin, Bill Ramsay, and Bob White to see how the program is going in their locations. As you know, Austin, the accounting people in those three locations are using the program. And from what I've heard, it is very effective.

Austin: O.K. Don, I'll talk to you later.

Austin made a decision to have John present the program to the accounting department. He also assigned him the special project of working with them to implement the program.

Two things happened shortly after. John presented the program and fell flat on his face because he was neither qualified nor prepared to implement it. The second thing that happened was that I was offered a job as personnel manager of Bendix Products Aerospace in South Bend, Indiana. Needless to say, I took the job and both John and I were happy!

This particular case illustrates the very important point that a manager and subordinates may look differently at the reasons for resentment and/or resistance. Chapter Six talks about empathy, the first key to managing change. The manager must understand the specific reasons for resentment and/or resistance and not assume it's such general reasons as "fear of the unknown."

Why People Accept or Welcome Change

While some people resent and/or resist change, others accept and welcome it. The degree to which these opposites occur depends on many factors. Some of the reasons for positive reaction to change are described in this section.

Personal Gain. When changes are made, some people may gain such things as the following:

- *Security.* They feel more secure in their job because of the change. Perhaps more of their skills will be used. This can be true in such areas as computer-aided design where an individual is more effective working with computers than using a pen to design on a drafting board.
- *Money.* They may get a salary increase, more benefits, an incentive or profit-sharing program, or more overtime.
- *Authority.* They may be promoted to a position of greater authority, or they may get a new boss who gives them more authority than they had under the previous boss. If they want more authority, this can create very positive reactions.
- *Status/prestige.* They may get a new title, a new office, or a special assignment that carries with it status and prestige.
- *Responsibility.* They may have a job change that provides a new responsibility, their boss may have assigned more responsibility, or they may have a new boss who assigns more responsibility than the previous one did.
- *Better working conditions.* They may get a new working schedule, new equipment, or other conditions that make the job easier or more enjoyable.
- *Self-satisfaction.* They may get new satisfaction or feeling of achievement because of the change. Perhaps the new job gives them more of a chance to use their abilities, or the boss may eliminate some of the obstacles that had prevented them from doing their best. This can be one of the most important reasons why people react positively to a change.
- *Better personal contacts.* They might be located in a place where they will have closer contact with influential people. This visibility is very important to some people.

- *Less time and effort.* The change may make their job easier and require less time and effort. For example, work simplification programs carry the slogan "Work smarter, not harder." It can reduce the physical effort required to do the job. Sometimes a physical move will provide a more convenient place or less travel time between home and work.

Provides a New Challenge. While some people look at a change negatively because it requires effort and perhaps risk, others will be eager for it because it provides a new challenge. Those who like a challenge react positively. Those who want to maintain the status quo react negatively.

Likes/Respects the Source. If people have a positive attitude toward the person or the department he/she represents, they will probably accept and even welcome the change. Vince Lombardi, former coach of the Green Bay Packers, had gained tremendous respect from his players because he was so successful. When he spoke, they listened and willingly accepted his decisions. (They also recognized that it was a good idea to accept his decision if they wanted to continue to be a Packer!)

Likes Manner. People who are asked to do things instead of told to do them may react very positively. Someone described the most important words in the English language as follows:

Five most important words: I am proud of you.
Four most important words: What is your opinion?
Three most important words: If you please.
Two most important words: Thank you.
One most important word: You (or possibly We).

The tone may have much to do with resentment or acceptance.

Reduces Boredom. A plant manager took me on a tour of a small manufacturing company that makes stereophones. Much of the work was monotonous and boring. All employees were asked if they'd like to learn other jobs and rotate periodically from one job to another for variety. About half said yes while the other half said no. Changes that are designed to reduce boredom will be welcomed by some but resisted and resented by others.

Provides Input. One of the most powerful approaches to get acceptance is to ask for input before the final decision is made. This is described in detail in Chapter Eight.

Desires Change. Some people will react to change by thinking or saying, "It's about time." In other words, they have been anxious for the change to occur.

Improves Future. Some changes will open up new avenues for future success in the organization. People will be provided with opportunities to show what they can do. Future possibilities include promotion, more money, more visibility, more recognition, and more self-satisfaction. People who see changes in this light will accept and even welcome the change.

Right Time. Some changes come at just the right time. For example, a change in overtime policy or procedure may provide employees with more overtime and a chance to make more money. If more money is needed to pay current bills or to buy a luxury item like a videorecorder or a boat or to take a vacation, the change will be welcomed. On the other hand, if the employee needs more time and leisure with the family instead of the money, he or she will resent and probably fight the change.

Mixed Reactions

In Chapter Two, a case study was presented that described a change from a functional organization to a product organization. The position of assistant general manager was created for each of the product lines. Instead of reporting directly to the general manager, heads of engineering and manufacturing would now report to the assistant general manager of one of the product lines. Because of this change, some people suffered personal loss and resented the change while others gained and welcomed it. Those who lost included the general manager who resigned because he lost his power and authority to run the division the way he felt it should be run. The engineering manager and manufacturing manager also lost half of their responsibility and authority. They became engineering manager and manufacturing manager of one of the product lines instead of for the entire division.

On the other hand, the men who had been assistant manager of engineering and plant superintendent gained because they became engineering manager and manufacturing manager respectively of one of the product lines. This put them on the same level with their former bosses so they were enthusiastic about the change.

This change did not affect the personnel manager, the controller, and the marketing manager. They neither gained nor lost from the decision. They probably had feelings positive or negative about the change or the way it came about, but they neither gained nor lost directly.

In the early 1970s, Sears Roebuck decided to build the tallest building in the world in the Loop of Chicago. They moved all of their people from South Homan Avenue on the Eisenhower Expressway to downtown Chicago. An analysis of the change reveals that some of the people lost such things as personal contact with friends and important people with whom they worked; money because transportation costs would be higher and meals would be more expensive; time because it would take longer to get back and forth to work; feeling of security and safety because their offices were moved from the first floor to the fiftieth floor; pleasant working conditions because their old, large comfortable office was changed to a new formal desk or office with little or no privacy; and a feeling of personal identity because they were one of thousands of employees who entered the building at 7:55 A.M. and jammed into elevators to take them to their floor.

At the same time, some employees were enthusiastic because they gained such things as improved working conditions because they got a new office with new furniture and pictures on the wall instead of the old crowded space in which they worked; a new outlook because they moved from the first floor without a decent view to the fiftieth floor where they could look out and see Lake Michigan and much of Chicago; new contacts with important people because of the location of their office; noontime enjoyment because they could walk down Michigan Avenue and shop or eat in a nice restaurant instead of being isolated at the old Sears location; time and money because transportation was more convenient to the new office than to the old office; and a feeling of pride for working in the Sears Tower, the tallest building in the world.

Other employees would have mixed feelings. They liked the noon shopping but didn't like the transportation situation with extra costs and time; they liked the view from the fiftieth floor but didn't like to feel the building move in the wind or to think about the danger if a fire occurred; they liked the new office but didn't like the fact it wasn't as private as the old office; or they were proud to work in the tallest building in the world but they hated to wait for elevators and to be jammed in when they finally arrived.

These two case studies illustrate an important point. When changes occur, there are apt to be three different kinds of reactions that depend on personal gain or loss. Some people will resent and possibly resist the change because they lose something. Some will accept and even welcome the change because they gain something. And some have mixed feelings or can care less because they neither gain nor lose, or because the gains and losses balance out.

Summary

It is not true that everybody resists change. Nor is it true that everybody accepts change. It depends on the specific change and how people view it. This chapter has considered various reasons why a change would be accepted and even welcomed by some people. Some of the reasons have to do with the personal loss or gain that will result from the change. Some of them are tangible such as money, working conditions, and authority. Others are intangible such as contacts, status, recognition, and feelings of importance and security. Some of the expected losses or gains may occur and others may never materialize. But acceptance or resistance will depend to a large extent on what people expect will happen. Optimists are apt to accept change while pessimists are apt to resent them because of the "fear of the unknown." Another reason relates to their attitude. If they like the manager and/or the way in which the change is introduced, they will accept and even welcome it. If they don't like or respect the manager, they will probably resent or resist it.

Probably the most significant reason why people will accept or welcome or will resent or resist a change is related to the word *participation*. Employees who have not been asked for their input are apt to resent or resist the change if they feel they could have contributed. "If they had asked me, I could have given them some good ideas concerning the change" expresses their feeling.

Employees who have been asked for ideas and suggestions will most likely react positively toward the change that is finally introduced. And it doesn't seem to depend on whether or not their ideas were used. Rather, it depends on whether or not their ideas were considered in deciding on the change. Obviously, if their ideas are used, they will be more enthusiastic. Or, if their ideas are never used, they will become discouraged and perhaps negative. But if managers consider their ideas and explain why their ideas were not used, they can achieve a high level of acceptance for the decision to change.

Managers who plan to introduce change should recognize that there will probably be three classes of employees: those who will resent or resist, those who will accept or welcome, and those who are neutral. Later chapters of this book will examine three keys for managing change—empathy (Chapter Six), communication (Chapter Seven), and participation (Chapter Eight).

Part II

ᘒᘒᘒᘒᘒᘒᘒᘒᘒᘒᘒᘒᘒᘒᘒᘒᘒᘒᘒᘒᘒᘒᘒᘒᘒᘒᘒ

Methods
for Managing Change

ᘒᘒᘒᘒᘒᘒᘒᘒᘒᘒᘒᘒᘒᘒᘒᘒᘒᘒᘒᘒᘒᘒᘒᘒᘒᘒᘒ

Part Two describes the methods and techniques that managers must know if they are going to be successful in managing change. In Chapter Five, a practical seven-step model is described. The steps are: (1) determining the need for change, (2) preparing a tentative plan, (3) analyzing probable reaction, (4) making a final decision, (5) establishing a timetable, (6) communicating the change, (7) implementing the change.

Chapter Six discusses empathy, the first key in managing change. It emphasizes the need to know who will be affected by a change and how they will react to it. Specific forms and procedures are provided for gathering this information. The chapter emphasizes that knowing how people will react is an important factor in the decision to make a change as well as the speed with which the change should be implemented.

Chapter Seven concerns communication, the second crucial factor in managing change. Although the importance of communicating well is recognized by virtually all managers, that awareness is rarely acted upon. This chapter describes specific communication methods and techniques to use to be sure people understand an impending change and the reasons for it. Empathy for those affected can help a manager know what information should be communicated.

Chapter Eight focuses on participation. Increasing numbers of organizations recognize that this is also a crucial element in managing change effectively. Being asked for input on a decision that affects them lets employees know that their point of view is being considered and generates a positive feeling toward the manager who proposes a change. In addition, their input will provide ideas to consider in defining the change and getting it implemented. Imposing changes on employees usually results in resistance. Involving employees in planning for change usually results in acceptance and even commitment on the part of those affected. This chapter provides details on the why and how of using participation most effectively.

Chapter Nine synthesizes the crucial points from the preceding three chapters and focuses on applying them in management situations. This chapter provides details on the why and how of employing empathy, communication, and participation in managing change effectively.

5

CIOIOIOIOIOIOIOIOIOIOIOIOIOIOIOIOIOIOIOIOIOIOIOIO

A Step-by-Step
Change Model

Steps in Change Process

In order to manage change effectively, a systematic approach is required. The following seven steps should be followed to ensure that the best decisions are made and that the changes will be accepted by those involved. This chapter will describe each step and illustrate how it may be implemented. The steps are summarized in Figure 2.

Step 1. Determining the Need or Desire for a Change. This can be done in many ways. For example, based on facts or feelings, top management can determine that there is a need for change. Or, a manager, either personally or based on suggestions from subordinates and/or others, can decide that there is a need for a change.

Some of the authors cited in Chapter Three offered the following suggestions on how this should be done: Lippitt (1981) suggests that a chance for all those who would be involved to participate in an assessment of the way things are and the way things might be is a very important aspect of a humane process of change. Luthans, Maciag, and Rosenkrantz (1983) suggest that behavior of people be observed in order to determine the need for change. Odiorne (1984) feels that the best option for change is one created by the people who must implement it, or one for which the implementers can claim owner-

Figure 2. A Manager's Model for Change.

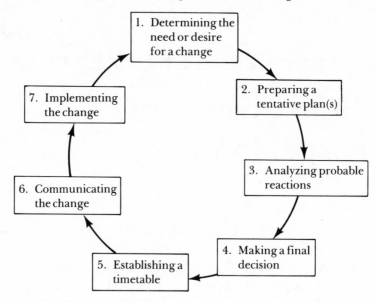

ship. Rogers (1962) stresses that before changes are made, it is essential that a thorough analysis be made of both the individual and the social system. The purpose of the analysis is to develop a complete diagnosis of the situation to help determine the program development strategies. Schaller (1978) suggests that a discrepancy must be identified between the current situation and the ideal. He states that the best approach is to have individuals identify this discrepancy themselves.

Step 2. Preparing a Tentative Plan(s). A tentative plan or plans should be developed in order to implement the change. The emphasis should be on the word *tentative,* which means "subject to change." It is important at this step that those who develop the tentative plan(s) are open to change and do not take a defensive attitude when reactions are negative and/or suggest a modification. To be open-minded at this point is a prerequisite for the effective implementation of the change. Otherwise, those who have other ideas will recognize that their input is not really being considered. The consequences will be a reluctance to speak freely as well as resentment for being asked without being listened to.

As in the first step, participation is a necessary process. Even before tentative plans are developed, those involved can be asked for their ideas. Brainstorming at this point can be very productive because it can elicit ideas that can be worked into tentative plans. It can also emphasize the fact that higher management *really* wants their input. Lippitt (1981) suggests that a manager brainstorm with the team to list all the steps of action that might be steps toward the good, including coping with the identified blocks.

Step 3. Analyzing Probable Reactions. Almost every proposed change will be met with three different types of reactions. Some people will resent and possibly resist the change if it is implemented. Some people will remain neutral—they could care less whether the change is made or not. And others will accept and possibly welcome the change. Details of these reactions were described in Chapter Four.

At this point it is important for managers to understand the individuals who will be involved. According to Bennett (1961, p. 3), "the attitude of a leader toward other persons is probably more critical than the nature of the change itself. The more person-centered a leader is in his approach to a change effort, the more he is likely to be seen by others as friendly and supportive." Rogers (1962) stresses that managers need to understand that individuals typically go through a five-step process of awareness, interest, evaluation, trial, and adoption. This need to know and understand the people will be discussed in Chapter Six.

Step 4. Making a Final Decision. The final decision should be made after a comparison of the plans and approaches that have been considered. The brainstorming described in step 2 can produce many options to consider. The reaction to tentative plans can also help in making a final decision.

Two possible approaches should be considered at this point. The first is for the manager to consider all the data and decide. This approach is quick and emphasizes the authority and status of the manager. If he or she is highly respected by subordinates, this approach can be effective. It can also be effective if the input from subordinates is used in making the decision. A high level of acceptance will also be achieved if the people will benefit from the decision.

The other approach is to use group problem solving. The manager would call together all or some of the people involved and say, "*We* are going to make a decision." This approach can be effective if the manager is able to conduct a productive meeting and get people to arrive at a consensus. It has the advantage of getting a high level of commitment to the decision by the subordinates because it was "our" decision rather than the decision by the manager. It sometimes results in animosity and unhappiness on the part of the subordinates because they can't agree. According to Bennett (1961, p. 3), "the process of change is helped when the person who will be affected can participate in the decision-making process. The greater the participation, the more assurance people have of being able to influence the direction and impact of the change and, consequently, to identify and resolve their personal resistance."

The critical aspect of this fourth step in the process is to arrive at the best possible decision with a high level of acceptance on the part of those involved.

Step 5. Establishing a Timetable. Sometimes, the change is a simple one and can be implemented in one step. Other changes may be complicated and require a timetable for the implementation.

According to Hersey and Blanchard (1972), there are two different change cycles known as "coerced" and "participative." The coerced cycle is fast while the participative cycle is slow and evolutionary. The disadvantage of the coerced cycle is that it can only be maintained as long as the leader has position power to make it stick. It often results in animosity, hostility and in some cases overt and covert behavior to undermine and overthrow. The main advantage of the participative style is that it tends to be long-lasting since the people are highly committed to the change. Margulies and Wallace (1973) caution that changes in behavior require time, nurturance and effort if they are to be incorporated as stabilized patterns of action. Meaningful and real change is a long-term endeavor.

The speed with which change is introduced may be as important as the change itself. If everyone is eager for the change, then the change should be implemented with as much speed as practical. If resistance is going to be strong, the change should be implemented slowly, possibly with the use of a pilot group or some similar approach.

The following example will illustrate some considerations that will determine the speed with which change is introduced: Your subordinates work on a line to assemble small radios. Each of them works at one of the six stations and does one sixth of the assembly for each radio. The worker then passes it on to the next person for the next operation. You have decided to enrich their jobs by having each worker assemble the entire radio and put his or her name on it. If you announced this plan to your subordinates, how would they react? (Select the one that best fits your situation.)

A.   All of them would welcome the change.
B.   Most of them would welcome the change.
C.   About half would welcome the change.
D.   Most of them would resist the change.
E.   All of them would resist the change.

If the answer is A, the change could be implemented as soon as it is possible to train the people and make the change in layout. If the answer is C or D, however, then the timetable should look something like this:

1.   Set up a pilot program for those who are in favor of the change. Train them and implement the change as soon as possible.
2.   Talk with those who are opposed to the change to determine why each person opposes the change.
3.   Based on the information gathered in step 2, proceed accordingly. For example, those who are afraid they will fail might be willing to perform three steps of the process instead of all six. They should be trained accordingly. Others may be allowed to stay on the present system until they

become receptive to the change. Upward communication and participation are also important at this stage. Operators can train each other and help make decisions regarding the speed and manner in which the change can be implemented. In most cases, the success of the change, the acceptance of those doing it, and time can turn resistance into acceptance.

Step 6. Communicating the Change. Although it is listed as step 6, communication is a continuous process that begins in step 1. It must be a two-way process—telling and selling the plan as well as listening to reactions and suggestions. When the final decision has been made and a timetable has been established, a thorough, planned communication approach is necessary. Chapter Seven will describe the process in detail.

Step 7. Implementing the Change. This is the action step in which the final decision is implemented according to the timetable established in step 5. Continuous evaluation is an integral part of this step. If the change is not proceeding as planned and resistance is evident, it is important to stop and evaluate the situation. The decision arrived at in step 4 should first be reviewed. Should the decision be modified? Should it be reconsidered? If it is still felt that it is the best decision, the timetable should then be analyzed. Is it being introduced too rapidly? Could the timetable be modified? The third consideration involves communications. Do people understand it? Do they have questions that should be answered? Finally, is there enough participation involved in the implementation? The answer to these questions will provide the information needed to get the decision implemented with maximum acceptance.

These seven steps are not as clear and distinct a sequence as Figure 2 illustrates. For example, steps 2 and 3 might be repeated several times before arriving at step 4. Or, step 3 may be inserted after step 5 to obtain reactions to a tentative timetable. As was mentioned, step 6 is a continuous process.

There is an underlying philosophy of participation in the entire model. It has been expressed strongly by many of the writers quoted in Chapter Three. It is so important in the process that Chapter Eight is devoted to it. Managers who don't believe in or practice a participatory style of leadership will never be able to get the quality of decisions and acceptance that can be achieved by involving subordinates and other people.

Case Study

The following case study illustrates the seven steps of the model.

Step 1. Determining the Need for a Change. At a meeting of the board of deacons at Elmbrook Church in Waukesha, Wisconsin, a decision was made to consider the reorganization of the church. Because of the continuing growth of the church and problems involving leadership, two major considerations were to be studied—the change from board of deacons to council of elders as the governing body and the change from election to appointment of the members of the governing body.

A "blue-ribbon" committee of ten people was formed consisting of three present deacons, five former deacons of which four were former chairmen of the board of deacons, and two pastors including the senior pastor. At its first meeting, the committee decided on two guiding principles: (1) Whenever possible, decisions would be based on the Bible. (2) The decisions that would be made would not be based on the present senior pastor. Rather, they would be made on the basis of what's best for Elmbrook Church on a long-range basis.

Step 2. Preparing a Tentative Plan. After careful study and discussion by the committee, a number of tentative decisions were reached:

1. The board of deacons would be replaced as the governing body by the council of elders consisting of twelve or more male members.

2. Deacons and deaconesses would be selected by pastors and leaders of the church. Their role would be as leaders and teachers. (This was the first time that women would serve as deaconesses.)

3. The elders would be selected by the members of the gov-

erning body. (This would replace the process by which
church leaders were elected by the membership.)

Step 3. Analyzing Probable Reactions. The committee and
the current board of deacons recognized that there were members of the congregation who would be strongly opposed to several of the recommendations: (1) the decision that elders must
be male, (2) the establishing of deaconesses, and (3) the change
from the election process to the selection process for picking
members of the governing body.

In recognizing this opposition, it was decided to communicate the tentative changes and to encourage members of the
congregation to ask questions and express their reactions, favorable or unfavorable. At the first open meeting on a Sunday evening, several members of the committee presented the recommendations and answered questions and listened to reactions,
favorable and unfavorable. At the second open meeting on a
Tuesday evening, several other members of the committee presented the recommendations and again welcomed comments
and reactions. At both of these meetings, opposition as well as
support to the proposal was expressed regarding the role of
women as well as the change from the election to appointment
of elders. In one of the meetings, an unofficial vote was taken
on both issues and the proposals of the committee were favored
three to one. In addition to these open meetings, members of
the committee offered to discuss the changes with individuals
and with small groups. A number of individuals and several
small groups took advantage of this offer.

The next step in the process was for the committee to
make a final recommendation to the board of deacons for approval. The proposal was approved and necessary constitutional
changes were prepared to implement the proposal. These changes
were communicated to the congregation in writing. Members of
the congregation were invited to offer in writing to the board of
deacons their suggested constitutional changes. Four · recommended changes were submitted.

Prior to the congregational meeting at which the proposed
constitutional changes would be voted on, written copies of the

four recommendations from the congregation as well as the recommendations from the board of deacons were mailed to all church members.

In planning the meeting agenda, the board of deacons wanted to be sure that all recommendations were fairly presented so that no one would feel that the recommendations from the board had been "railroaded" through. Therefore, the following agenda was planned and implemented:

1. The present organization of the church was presented.
2. The proposed changes from the board of deacons were presented.
3. The four proposed changes from the congregation were presented by the individuals who had developed them.
4. Questions were encouraged and open discussion was held on all the proposals.
5. The proposed changes were voted on in the reverse order in which they had been presented. The vote on the changes recommended by the board of deacons was presented last. Votes were made by the raising of hands.

Step 4. Making a Final Decision. Approximately 1,200 of the 2,500 members attended the meeting. None of the first four proposals received more than 100 votes. The changes that were recommended by the board of deacons received approximately 1,000 votes, far more than the necessary two thirds.

Although a few people felt that the congregation had made a serious mistake in approving all of the changes recommended by the board of deacons, no one felt that the decision was made unfairly. The resistance to the changes was greatly minimized by the approach that was taken in introducing the changes and getting them approved. Effective communication was one of the keys. The committee made sure that everyone understood the proposed changes and the reasons for them. Also, everyone had a chance to ask questions and render their opinions. Members of the committee as well as deacons listened to comments before making a final decision regarding the proposed changes. In addition, members were invited to put in writing and orally present their recommendations to the congregational meeting. This carefully planned approach accomplished the two objectives of the changes: to make the changes that would be best for Elmbrook Church and to get them accepted by the membership.

Step 5. Establishing a Timetable. Because the acceptance level was so high, it was decided to implement the new policies and procedures immediately.

Step 6. Communicating the Change. The tentative plan had been carefully and completely communicated in the process of making a decision. Several meetings were held to explain the plan and answer questions. Also, upward communication had been encouraged, even where it was dramatically opposed to the tentative plan that the task force had developed. Those who resisted the plan were not only encouraged to present their plan in writing but also to present it orally at the congregational meeting. Every attempt was made to be sure everyone in the congregation understood the proposed plan as well as the ideas of those who opposed it.

Step 7. Implementing the Change. The plan was implemented without delay. Nearly everyone accepted it. Most of the people welcomed it because they felt it was a good change. Others accepted it because they didn't really care, one way or another. Some who originally opposed it accepted it because of the manner in which it was introduced. Others were influenced by peer pressure.

The only observable negative reaction came from one church family that strongly resisted it. The father had presented one of the opposing plans. In his statement concerning the plan that the committee had recommended, he referred to it as "committing church suicide" if it was adopted. Shortly after the committee's plan had been ratified and his plan had been rejected, he and his family left to join another church.

Summary

The model described in Figure 2 provides a practical way for managers to manage change. It begins with a determination of need and ends with the implementation of the change. Critical elements include empathy (analyzing probable reactions), communication, and participation. The objective of the model is to implement the best possible change with the greatest degree of acceptance on the part of those involved. The following chapters will illustrate the ways and means for accomplishing the objective.

6

OIOIOIOIOIOIOIOIOIOIOIOIOIOIOIOIOIOIOIOIOIOIO

Empathy:
The First Key
to Successful Change

In implementing the model described in Chapter Five, there are three important concepts that become the keys to the successful management of change. These are empathy, communication, and participation. This chapter will discuss empathy. The next two will focus on communication and participation.

A practical definition of empathy is "putting yourself in the shoes of the other person." I know of a production foreman who took the words literally. When a worker wanted to talk to him about a problem, he would say, "I want to be sure that I understand your problem and I also want to be sure you understand my position." So, after the worker had explained the problem and he had explained his position, he and the worker exchanged chairs. Each one explained what he understood the other person had said. If there was misunderstanding, they expressed themselves again until both were able to put themselves in the shoes of the other. An old Indian proverb described it by saying, "Don't criticize a person until you have walked in his moccasins."

I have often asked fishermen, "What is the most important quality of a successful fisherman?" The most frequent answer is "patience." The correct answer is "empathy"—the ability to put one's self in the place of the fish, to know where they are and what they are most apt to bite on at that particular time.

In managing change, the first key is to know to what extent the change will be resented or rejected on the one hand and accepted or welcomed on the other hand. If everyone is enthused about it, it is probably wise to proceed immediately. But if it will be resented and resisted, it is probably wise to reconsider the decision and/or go slowly in order to get it accepted.

In order to be accurate in analyzing the degree of resistance or acceptance, it is necessary to consider each person individually. The better a manager knows the individuals who will be affected by the change, the more accurate will be his or her analysis of their reactions toward it.

Get to Know Your Employees

The Know Factor Ballot, Exhibit 1, is a practical tool for getting to know the most important things. The first step is to put a check mark in one of the three columns after each item. This will answer the question "Which factors are most important to know?" The next step is to insert the "Very Important" items in the column headings in the form shown in Exhibit 2, "Empathy Worksheet." In the example, items 1, 4, 5, 6, 7, 11, 15, and 17 were selected. The third step is to insert the names of subordinates in the spaces under "Name." The fourth step is to ask the question "Do I know this about the individual?" If the answer is yes, and X should be placed in the appropriate square. If the answer is no, the space should be left blank. An analysis of the completed form will clearly indicate the important factors that are known and those that should be learned.

The final step is to learn the important factors that are not known. This can be done by looking at personnel files, asking questions, listening, and observing. One way to approach the learning is to set a goal for each month. The goal might be to get to know one or two persons better. Or the goal for a month might be to learn the "Ambitions and Goals" of all the employees.

When a change is contemplated or decided on, the form entitled "Empathy Regarding Change," Exhibit 3, should be completed. For each person who will be affected by the change, an X should be inserted in the appropriate space. If the reaction

Exhibit 1. "Know Factor" Ballot.

	Very Important	Important	Not Important
1. Name and nickname			
2. Home (where he or she lives; owns or rents)			
3. Status (married or single)			
4. Formal Education (how much, where)			
5. Work experience (where, type of work)			
6. Outside hobbies and activities			
7. Health (disabilities, problems)			
8. Children (names, ages, achievements)			
9. Religion—background and present affiliation			
10. Politics—preference and activities			
11. Attitudes (toward company, boss, union)			
12. Problems outside the plant			
13. Friends at the plant			
14. Financial situation			
15. Ambitions and goals			
16. War experience			
17. Personality (introvert, extrovert)			
18. Intelligence			
19. Birthday			
20. Date of employment			
21. Social and cultural background			
22. Continuing Education (seminars, workshops, and so on)			
23.			
24.			
25.			

Exhibit 2. Empathy Worksheet.

NAME	MUST KNOW FACTORS							
	Name and Nickname	Education	Experience	Outside Activities	Health	Attitudes	Ambitions and Goals	Personality
RALPH HAFFEE	X	X	X	X		X		X
TIM RYDER	X		X			X		X
MARY POLLACK	X	X	X			X		X
BARBARA BURRELL	X							X
MIKE PROKOP	X	X				X		X
ED SAUNDERS	X	X		X		X		X

is not known, it must be determined. Sometimes the best approach is to ask the individual. At other times, a more indirect approach such as observing, listening, or talking to others may be the best approach.

Example

In the following example, you are asked to use empathy to determine how your subordinates would react to the type of changes described.

Suppose that you are the manager in the following situation involving job rotation. Each of your people knows how to do one job in your department. You have decided to train each of them to do three different jobs. You are going to have them rotate jobs so they would do a different job each day for three

Exhibit 3. "Empathy Regarding Change" Form.

Change being considered:

Key: R_1 = Resist A = Accept
R_2 = Resent W = Welcome
N = Neutral ? = Not sure

NAME	R_1	R_2	N	A	W	?	COMMENTS (Reason, etc.)
RALPH HAFFEE			X				Won't affect him positively or negatively
TIM RYDER					X		Has suggested the change
MARY POLLACK						X	Don't know how she will react
BARBARA BURRELL		X					Will probably resent it because she hasn't been consulted
MIKE PROKOP	X						He will lose some status and security
ED SAUNDERS				X			He will go along with it

days and then start the cycle again. How would they react? (Select the answer that best fits your situation.)

A. All of them would welcome the change.
B. Most of them would welcome the change.
C. About half would welcome the change.
D. Most of them would resist the change.
E. All of them would resist the change.

Your answer would depend on an individual analysis as described in Exhibit 3.

The answer to this example might be quite different than the example of job enrichment that was given on page 105. In that example, the job changed from a relaxed, secure situation to one where competition and complete responsibility were involved. This would create insecurity on the part of some employees. The example of job rotation provides variety but does not create the competition and complete responsibility that were involved in the job enrichment change.

The exercise you went through in analyzing these two situations is what you should do every time a change is contemplated or decided on. It will guide in both the decision regarding the change and in the implementation of it to get maximum acceptance.

Summary

The first key in any change situation is to use empathy to determine probable reaction to a contemplated or decided-on change. Empathy is not an inherited trait. It is something that can be developed by getting to know the other person. A systematic approach for getting to know that person is needed. Then, an analysis of and/or conversation with each affected person would reveal the degree to which he or she resents/resists or accepts/welcomes a change. This analysis will help to determine whether or not the change should be made as contemplated as well as the speed with which the change should be implemented. It will also provide clues for the second and third keys—communication and participation—that will be described in the next two chapters.

7

OIOIOIOIOIOIOIOIOIOIOIOIOIOIOIOIOIOIOIOIOIOIOIOIOI

Communication:
The Second Key
to Successful Change

It should not be surprising to any manager that communication is one of the keys to the management of change. It may be surprising, however, to learn that communication means more than "telling"; it means "creating understanding." This definition provides a real challenge to be sure it is accomplished.

Prerequisites to Communication

Before answering the questions of to whom, when, and how, it is important to look at the barriers that can exist between sender and receiver. An understanding of barriers as described in *No-Nonsense Communication* (Kirkpatrick, 1983) can give a manager some insight into approaches that will overcome the barriers.

Barriers can be divided into two parts—those that relate to the sender and those that relate to receivers. Those that are significant regarding change include the following:

Sender Barriers.

1. Sender doesn't know enough about the receiver.
2. Sender has a negative attitude toward message—doesn't want to communicate it.

3. Sender has a negative attitude toward the receiver.
4. Sender has a negative attitude toward communicating—doesn't care whether receiver understands or not.
5. Sender fails to get the attention and interest of the receiver.
6. Sender has poor communication skills (oral expression and/or writing).
7. Sender picks the wrong time.
8. Sender uses the wrong method.
9. Sender chooses the wrong place.
10. Sender uses vocabulary that isn't clear to the receiver (ambiguous and/or technical).
11. Sender doesn't communicate the right amount of information (too little or too much).
12. Sender uses negative tone.
13. Sender is in a hurry.
14. Sender fails to verify whether receiver understands.

Managers need to look at themselves as senders and recognize which of these barriers exist in a change situation. Their communication approach should then be planned to overcome or eliminate the barriers.

Receiver Barriers.

1. Receiver is preoccupied with something "more important."
2. Receiver doesn't like/respect the sender.
3. Receiver is not interested in the message.
4. Receiver "knows" what the message is going to be (or thinks so).
5. Receiver doesn't want to understand (message is unpleasant).
6. Receiver has emotional barriers (fear, anxiety, anger, frustration).
7. Receiver is physically tired.
8. Receiver is thinking about what to say when the sender finishes.
9. Receiver is distracted.

10.   Receiver pretends to listen when not listening.
11.   Receiver pretends to understand when doesn't understand.

Empathy is necessary in order to realize which of these barriers exist when changes are made. Communication approaches must be planned to overcome or eliminate the barriers.

Rapport. Rapport between sender and receiver is an important prerequisite to effective communication. They must have a good working relationship of mutual respect and trust. This can be illustrated by the following example. Thomas Samuel, a missionary in India, is trying to convert Hindus to Christianity. In order to get people to listen to him, he has to build relationships filled with friendship and trust. In order to do this, he lives among them. He has established schools to educate their children and a small hospital to take care of the sick. In addition, at Christmas, he invites people from nearby villages to a "love feast" where he provides food and clothing. He shows his love for them, in both practical and spiritual ways. And when he preaches a Christian message, they listen.

To Whom?

Who should be told about a change? The obvious answer is "those who need to know." A better answer is "those who need to know plus those who want to know." In other words, the change should be communicated to those who are concerned as well as those who are involved. When a change is contemplated or planned, the manager should make a list of those who should be informed. When in doubt, communicate. It is better to overcommunicate instead of undercommunicate. It is better to have some people saying, "I don't know why they told me, I could care less" than it is to have people say, "Why didn't they tell me? They don't tell me anything around here." The latter can create a negative attitude that could spread from this employee to others. Someone once said, "One rotten apple in a bushel will spoil the entire bushel." This philosophy can apply to a department, if the employee with the bad attitude feels strongly enough about it.

When?

"When?" is a difficult question to answer unless we use the phrase "whenever practical." Here, the word *practical* refers to the particular situation and implies that all factors must be considered.

For example, in South Bend in 1963, an article appeared in the local paper stating that Studebaker Corporation had put all of its employees on a one-month layoff from December 15 to January 15 without pay. It also stated that the employees were not informed of the layoff until just before quitting time on December 14. The reporter was very critical of the company for doing such a terrible thing just before Christmas without giving employees advance notice so they could adjust their Christmas spending accordingly.

The reporter's comments made sense to me. To check on the situation, however, I called the director of industrial relations (DIR) and asked whether the story was true, and if true, why he had given the workers such short notice. This was his answer: "Don, do you realize the working relationship between management and the union employees? Do you realize the negative employee attitudes that exist toward the company? We didn't dare give them any notice because we were afraid of what they would do. They would have been so mad that they would probably have taken it out on our product and equipment by damaging the cars on the assembly line and even destroying some of the equipment. We couldn't afford to let that happen."

This sad story illustrates the importance of the word *practical.* In general, it's a good policy to provide ample advance notice of change—whether the change is favorable or unfavorable. Managers must build a reputation for being honest, for letting their people know what is going to happen. And even if the news is bad, the information should not be held back. From the time the change is announced until the time it is implemented, continuous two-way communication should take place. Subordinates should be allowed to vent their feelings, ask questions, and offer reactions and suggestions. Managers should listen empathetically and provide answers and information as requested.

The answer to "When?" also is related to the question "To whom?" It is important for bosses to get information before subordinates. It is also important for managers to get information before officers of the union. There are two reasons for this. One has to do with feelings. Managers who get information from their bosses instead of from subordinates or through the grapevine feel important. They feel they belong. They feel that they are part of management. This is especially critical in regard to first-level supervisors who often feel that they are not part of management. The second reason for providing information through channels is that bosses can prepare answers to questions that come from subordinates.

There is one other person who should probably receive information before the rank-and-file workers. This person is the "natural leader" to whom the other employees turn for information, advice, and counsel. This "natural leader," probably one of the nonmanagement employees, is in a position to influence the level of acceptance on the part of the other workers. He or she is a person you want on your side. And it is important to capitalize on the natural leadership that he or she has earned.

How?

Which is better, written or oral communication? The answer, of course, is that it all depends on the situation. Sometimes written is better, while oral will be more effective at other times. Here are some of the reasons why each is better in certain situations.

Use *oral (face-to-face) communication* when:

1. The receiver is not particularly interested in getting the message. Oral provides more opportunities for getting and keeping interest and attention.
2. It is important to get feedback. It's easier to get feedback by observing facial expressions and asking questions.
3. Emotions are high. Oral provides more opportunity for both sender and receiver to let off steam, cool down, and create a suitable climate for understanding.

4. Receiver is too busy or preoccupied to read. Oral provides better opportunity to get attention.
5. Criticism of receiver is involved. Oral provides more opportunity to accomplish this without arousing resentment. Also, oral is less threatening because it has not been formalized in writing. Written communication is not private (at least as receiver sees it) even though it might be marked "Personal and Confidential."
6. Sender wants to persuade or convince. Oral provides more flexibility, opportunity for emphasis, chance to listen, and opportunity to remove resistance and change attitudes.
7. Oral is more natural. For example, in most cases it is more natural to give instructions orally rather than writing them out. Likewise, it is more natural to communicate orally with someone who has a desk next to you or who is in an office a few feet from your own.
8. Discussion is needed. A complicated subject frequently requires discussion to be sure of understanding.
9. Receiver can't read the language of the sender. Some people can understand a spoken foreign language but can't read it.

Use *written communication* when:

1. The sender wants a record for future references.
2. The receiver will be referring to it later.
3. The message is complex and requires study by the receiver.
4. The message includes a step-by-step procedure.
5. A copy of the message should go to another person.

How Would You Communicate? To illustrate the appropriate use of written and oral communication, the following is a list of some changes that managers might make in their department. In front of each, indicate by a *W* (written), *O* (oral), or both *W* and *O* how you as a manger could communicate.

_____ 1. A change in the method of assembling parts (communicate to the assemblers).

_____ 2. A change in the policy regarding "wash-up

time" at the close of the shift (communicate to those affected).

_____ 3. A change in the way that time cards will be made out to provide information for the computer (communicate to workers who must complete the time cards).

_____ 4. A change in the labor agreement that has just been negotiated with the union (communicate to foremen who supervise the hourly union employees).

_____ 5. A change in the incentive system involving the pay of each employee (communicate to those affected).

_____ 6. The introduction of a new pension plan that requires employees to contribute (communicate to each employee who is eligible).

_____ 7. A change in the pension plan from contributory to noncontributory (communicate to those affected).

_____ 8. The introduction of a compulsory safety glass policy (communicate to foremen and supervisors who must implement the policy).

_____ 9. The introduction of robots to replace some of the old machines and reduce the number of workers (communicate to foremen and supervisors in departments where the robots will be installed).

_____ 10. An announcement that the company has been purchased by a large conglomerate (communicate to managers at all levels).

_____ 11. A new procedure for picking new foremen and supervisors (communicate to the plant manager who has had complete control for picking foremen).

_____ 12. A simple change in organization structure and reporting relationships (communicate to all employees).

To make decisions regarding these twelve situations, it is necessary to analyze the advantages and disadvantages of oral and written communication and apply them to each situation. Here are my recommendations regarding the twelve situations and the rationale for each:

W and O   1.   *A change in the method of assembling parts.* This change requires a complete understanding as well as training in how to do it. Therefore, *O* is necessary because both telling and showing are required. In addition, a written description should be available for possible reference by assemblers and also by those who may be interested but need not know how to do it.

W and O   2.   *A change in policy regarding wash-up time.* To get understanding and acceptance, it is important to tell the people personally and encourage them to ask questions and react. Therefore, oral is necessary. In addition, because it is a new policy, it should be written.

W and O   3.   *A change in the way that time cards will be made out.* It is important to explain the reasons for the change as well as the change itself. Opportunity for questions and discussion should be provided. Therefore, oral is necessary. It would also be important to provide a sample of a newly completed card (written) to help employees understand the change.

W and O   4.   *A change in the labor agreement.* Obviously, supervisors and foremen will need a copy of the new contract (written). It would probably be a good idea also to provide a separate written summary of the new clauses or new interpretations of the old clauses (written). However, this isn't enough. In the first place, most of the foremen would probably not read the new contract, and if they read it, many would not understand it. Therefore it is necessary to use oral to explain the clauses and answer questions. A group meeting is probably the best way to do it. It might be advisable to hand out a copy of the changes before the meeting and encourage the foremen to read it. Some will and some won't, but it will help to achieve understanding. A short quiz might be introduced to see whether or not they understand.

W and O   5.   *A change in the incentive system.* Oral is critical because there is so much emotion involved. The new program must be explained clearly and completely and reactions encouraged. Questions must be answered completely. In addition, it is probably a good idea to describe it in writing and put it on the bulletin board so all employees can see it. This will help answer questions and straighten out disagreements that may come up later.

W and O   6.   *A new contributory pension plan.* Employees must understand the plan. If only stated in writing, it is almost certain that misunderstanding will occur. So oral presentations and discussions must be held.

The story is told about a small organization that was going to introduce such a plan. It required the participation of all employees. It was an excellent plan from the employer's standpoint because their contribution would cover only 20 percent of the premium.

Top management first explained it to all the managers. After free and open discussion, it was determined that each manager clearly understood it. Each manager was then instructed to communicate to all subordinates to get understanding and to have them sign the participation card. All employees signed up for the program except Joe, a sixty-year-old with thirty-five years' experience with the company. When the foreman couldn't get him to sign, the superintendent talked to him, explained the program, and asked him to sign the card. Joe refused. The plant manager then went to Joe, explained the benefits, and told him that all the other employees had signed up but that 100 percent participation was needed or the plan couldn't be implemented. He politely asked Joe to sign. Joe politely refused by saying, "I don't believe in this. I think each person should take care of his own future. I don't think the company should pay most of the premium. I've set aside money for my retirement and I think every other employee should do the same."

The plant manager then went to the president of the company and explained the situation. The president was furious and said, "I'll go talk to Joe myself."

President: Joe, I understand that the foreman, the superintendent, and the plant manager have all explained the insurance program to you and that you've refused to sign. Now here's the card. *Sign or you are fired!*

Joe: Let's see now, where do you want me to sign?

President: Right there where the X is.

Joe: O.K.

President (puzzled): Joe, I don't understand why did you sign now but didn't sign when the other three guys asked you to?

Joe: Well, I guess it's the first time I really understood it.

W   7. *A change in the pension plan from contributory to noncontributory.* This change will obviously receive positive reaction because it will be of benefit to all employees. Therefore, written will probably suffice. Managers should be available to answer any questions that come up.

W and O   8. *A compulsory safety glass policy.* Foremen and supervisors must not only understand the policy but must be convinced that it is necessary. Therefore, discussion must be held to answer questions and counteract objections. Because it is a policy, it should be written so it can be analyzed and discussed and also because all policies should be written.

O   9. *The introduction of robots.* The introduction of any automated equipment must be understood and accepted. Oral presentations are needed for explanation and questions and reactions should be solicited. In this case, the communication is to those who will supervise the installation of the robots and live with the results. Complete information should be provided regarding the possible replacement or transfer of people, procedures for retraining those who will operate the robots, and other ramifications.

O   10. *Purchase of the company.* Whenever an organization is going to be purchased or "taken over" by another organization, it is necessary to communicate as completely as possible. Oral presentation is necessary to be followed by questions and answers. Obviously there will be questions that can't be answered because management does not know the answers. These questions have to do with the changes that will result from the takeover. Managers should not be afraid to say, "We don't know but we'll keep you informed as we get more information." And they must remember and keep that promise.

O   11. *A new procedure for picking new foremen.* In this situation, the decision has been made by top management and must be communicated to the head of manufacturing, who will probably have a negative or at least defensive reaction to a new procedure that takes away some of his/her authority. Therefore, an oral explanation of the new procedure as well as the rationale are necessary. Also, his/her reactions must be obtained and answers given to questions and concerns. If the new procedure is not finalized, the input of the manufacturing manager should be considered and modifications made if it will improve the quality and/or the acceptance of the decision. It is pretty obvious that the new procedure will not be implemented successfully if the head of manufacturing wants to sabotage it or even if he or she lacks the enthusiasm to carry it out.

W   12. *A simple organizational change.* If the change is simple and of general interest without a lot of emotion involved, a written notice can suffice. It should be given to all managers first and then posted on bulletin boards throughout the plant. The announcement should indicate the source of the change (general manager, personnel manager, and so on) as well as the person to contact (personnel manager, your supervisor, and so on) if there are any questions.

These twelve situations have challenged you to think through various types of change and plan how you would communicate them. There were two reasons for inserting this exercise in this chapter. In the first place, it gave you practice in analyzing situations and deciding how to communicate. This practice should continue in your real job situations. Secondly, it emphasizes the situations in which "oral" and "written" are better. It also indicated that in most situations it is probably a good idea to use both. And it also indicated that in most instances, written is not enough because it may not be read and understood and also because it does not provide the right climate for response and discussion.

Whenever possible, information should go directly from sender to receiver, whether written or oral is used. The following example illustrates the problem with "passing it on."

> A colonel gave this message to his executive officer: "Tomorrow evening at approximately 20:00 hours, Halley's Comet will be visible in this area, an event that occurs only once every seventy-five years. Have the men fall out in the battalion area in fatigues, and I will explain the rare phenomenon to them. In case of rain, we will not be able to see anything, so assemble the men in the theater and I will show them films of it."
>
> The executive officer told the company commander: "By order of the colonel, tomorrow at 20:00 hours, Halley's Comet will appear above the battalion area. If it rains, fall the men out in fatigues. Then march to the theater where this rare phenomenon will take place, something that occurs only once every seventy-five years."
>
> The company commander told the lieutenant: "By order of the colonel, in fatigues at 20:00 hours tomorrow evening, the phenomenal Halley's Comet will appear in the theater. In case of rain in the battalion area, the colonel will give another order, something that occurs every seventy-five years."
>
> The lieutenant told the sergeant: "Tomorrow at 20:00 hours, the colonel will appear in the theater with Halley's Comet, something that happens every seventy-five years. If it rains, the colonel will order the comet into the battalion area."
>
> The sergeant told the squad: "When it rains tomorrow at 20:00 hours, the phenomenal seventy-five-year-old General Halley, accompanied by the colonel, will drive his Comet through the battalion area in fatigues."

Feedback

Feedback is a necessary part of the communication process. It means more than asking, "Are there any questions?" It means that people will "feed back" to management their understanding of what they have read and heard. It also means that people will "feed back" their reactions, feelings, comments, and suggestions regarding any change that has been planned or implemented.

In order to get this feedback, it is necessary to build rapport between managers who are ready, willing, and able to listen to subordinates, whether the reactions are positive or negative. Feedback also requires managers to refrain from being defensive, even if the comments are deragatory. Empathic and nondefensive listening are critical. Subordinates must feel free to speak freely and frankly.

There are several reasons why feedback is important. First of all, it may provide some good ideas for making decisions regarding the proposed change. If the change decision has already been made, ideas may be received regarding the implementation of the change. Another reason for soliciting and listening to feedback has to do with the feelings of employees. If they feel their reactions and suggestions are being listened to and considered, they will be more apt to accept and even welcome the change.

Summary

It probably isn't necessary to point out that communication is one of the three keys in managing change. Every manager knows that. But it is important to call attention to the following aspects of communication that are frequently misunderstood or often ignored by managers.

- *Definition. Communicate* means to "create understanding" and not merely to send. If people don't understand, the manager has not communicated.
- *To Whom.* The criteria for deciding to whom to communicate should include those who *want* to know as well as those who *need* to know.
- *When.* Care should be taken regarding the timing of the communication. First of all, managers should be told before nonmanagers and union officers get the information. Secondly, those who will be affected should be told as far in advance as practical."

- *How.* Managers should give thought to the method of communicating before doing it. It is important to understand the advantages and disadvantages of oral and written communication. When making a decision, it is also important to use empathy as described in Chapter Six. In most cases, oral as well as written may be necessary to get understanding as well as to gain acceptance. In very few cases will written communication alone do the job.

The importance of effective communication and the seriousness of misunderstanding can be illustrated by the following example. The village blacksmith hired a young man who was eager to work long, hard hours at low pay in order to learn the trade. The blacksmith wanted to train his new employee at once, so he started with this instruction: "Now listen carefully and do *exactly* as I say. When I take the hot iron from the fire, I'll place it on the anvil; then when I nod my head, you strike *it* with this hammer." The young man did exactly as he was told, according to *his* understanding. Now he's the new village blacksmith.

8

ОІО

Participation:
The Third Key
to Successful Change

Empathy, the first key, requires a manager to determine feelings and reactions toward a change. Communication, the second key, requires the manager to maintain continuous, complete, and clear communication with all persons affected by the change. The third key, participation, requires a manager to get involvement from those concerned with and affected by the change.

History of Participative Management

As early as 1958, participative management existed in some organizations. A well-known men's apparel manufacturing company was faced with the necessity of modernizing its production methods to meet competition. This involved a complete changeover from the batch process to the "continuous-flow" process, which meant reengineering the whole assembly line and introducing some automatic processes. Major innovations were planned by a firm of engineering consultants.

Despite good labor-management relations, there was a long history of resistance to change among the 800 employees in the three plants. To meet this, the company had evolved a system of participative management by encouraging interactive discussions between management and workers to the optimum degree. In this instance, the technical nature of the predetermined changes limited full participation in the initial stages of the changeover.

The changes were introduced and developed in the two smaller company plants on a somewhat experimental basis. Group meetings were held in which workers performing the same operation met with local management. The changes were announced, objectives given, and stress placed on the underlying economic necessity. Workers were assured their income level would be maintained. Frank and open discussion was encouraged.

Immediately afterwards, the technical innovations were introduced gradually on the production floor. Experts showed and instructed the operators while engineers and supervisors watched, asked, and answered questions. As problems arose, they were discussed informally. As new methods were mastered, other changes were introduced.

A second series of group meetings was called to discuss and revise wage rates. Management explained its subsidy program designed to protect earnings in the readjustment period and listened in order to remedy all complaints. Back on the production floor, individual consultations continued. Senior operators interviewed the workers to uncover any remaining technical problems and bring them forward for solution.

Finally, with the new system in full swing, management decided to use the same approach in the large plant where the changes were effected more rapidly.

The following results had been accomplished after one year:

- Productivity levels increased 10 percent.
- Direct labor costs decreased 10 percent.
- Turnover and absenteeism declined.

The following factors were responsible for the success:

1. Management's honest attempt to maximize worker participation.
2. Plans for change disclosed in interactive discussions (that is, management and worker).

3. Workers ideas given full and immediate consideration.
4. Earning levels protected by subsidy.
5. Management's determination to exert and maintain its *right to decide* within a policy of fairness and openness.

A research study was conducted by Lester Coch and John R. P. French, Jr. (1948), in a clothing factory. It deserves special comment because it is one of the most systematic studies of the phenomenon of resistance to change that has been made in a factory setting. The two researchers worked with four different groups of factory operators who were being paid on a modified piece-rate basis. For each of these four groups a minor change in the work procedure was installed by a different method, and the results were carefully recorded to see what, if any, problems of resistance occurred. The four experimental groups were roughly matched with respect to efficiency ratings and degree of cohesiveness. In each group the proposed change modified the established work procedure to about the same degree toward the supervisors, and there were no quits during the experimental period.

The researchers conclude that resistance to method changes could be overcome by *getting the people involved in the change to participate in making it.*

Emphasis on participation has become greater and greater. In the late 1960s and early 1970s, such books as Likert's (1967) *The Human Organization,* Myers's (1970) *Every Employee a Manager,* and Marrow's (1972) *The Failure of Success* stressed the need for participation. Most of the writers in Chapter Three of this book have stressed its importance. The Japanese approach to participative management, quality control circles, has been copied by many U.S. firms. In Cincinnati, a professional society called the International Association of Quality Circles has grown from the Japanese practice. This society is currently expanding its activities to all types of participative approaches. Its membership continues to grow and its national conferences continue to attract large crowds from all types and sizes of organizations. (See Chapter Thirteen for examples of the implementation of "quality circles.")

According to Eugene J. Catabiani, executive vice-president

of Westinghouse Electric's Power Generation Group (*Behavioral Sciences Newsletter*, 1983b, p. 3)

> The great hierarchical structures which were once thought to express the essence of America's managerial genius are being disassembled. An addiction to numbers and pure logic are being displaced by a new reverence for the human element. Today's emphasis on "running lean" presents a major management challenge. But running lean can be successful only if there is a cultural change, not just a cutback in numbers. And that, he said, is where participative management comes in. Participative management is most of all a way of releasing the natural, inherent enthusiasm and creativity of the entire organization.
>
> Change is not only a challenge to the participative manager, it is also a valuable tool. An environment of change—either initiated by a top manager or thrust in from the world outside—is helpful in encouraging the art of participative management. In the stormy sea of change, all managers in a particular group can sense themselves aboard the same boat. A spirit of mutual support in pursuit of survival can actually be sensed in the group. That's a good climate for team building. A good participative manager cherishes change, whatever its source.

In her book, *The Change Masters*, Kanter (1983, p. 241) states, "Involving grass-roots employees on participative teams with control over their own outcome helps the organization to get and use more ideas to improve performance and increase future skills. Whether called 'task forces,' 'quality circles,' 'problem-solving groups,' or 'shared-responsibility teams,' such vehicles for greater participation at all levels are an important part of an innovating company."

The Need for a Participative Management Philosophy

An effective participative program must be based on a philosophy that the input of employees can contribute to the effectiveness of an organization as well as achieve quality of work life and personal satisfaction for the employees. When the

Japanese firm Nissan Motor Company began building a new light truck factory in Smyrna, Tennessee, they counted on U.S. managers to run the plant. In selecting managers at all levels, they were very careful to pick those who believed in participative management. They realized that participative methods such as quality circles would not be effective unless top executives and the other managers believed in a participative philosophy. The managers had to believe that the input of employees was necessary, both for the success of the organization as well as the personal satisfaction of the employees. In other words, participative management was a way of life. And they implemented the philosophy with specific techniques that showed the workers that their opinions really did matter.

The president of Goodyear Aerospace told his plant managers that he believed in EI (employee involvement) and he expected them to do the same and implement the philosophy in their organization. At the new Fiero plant of Pontiac Motor, Division of General Motors, W. Edward Deming was hired as a consultant. He had become famous as the person who had done most to help the Japanese improve their quality image. Based on his recommendations, the managers of Pontiac, beginning at the top, changed their decision-making style. The traditional way had been for a manager to make a decision and then inform the subordinates. The new approach was to get input from subordinates and arrive at a consensus. All managers received training in this participative approach.

Participation and Decision Making

Professor Norman Maier (1963) of the University of Michigan pointed out the importance of participation when he identified three styles of leadership when making decisions. He described three ways in which managers make decisions:

1. The manager decides and tells or sells subordinates on the decision.
2. The manager asks for input from subordinates and then decides and tells or sells subordinates on his/her decision.

3.   The manager serves as a leader in getting subordinates to agree on a decision.

The first approach is nonparticipative. The second and third illustrate different levels of participation. In the first two approaches, the manager maintains control. The second approach may add to the quality of the decision by increasing the number of ideas under consideration. It will probably add to the acceptance also because people have had a chance to present their ideas.

The third approach is different than the second because it is truly a group decision. In the second approach, the leader gets all the "votes." In the third approach, he or she gets only one "vote." This third approach has some obvious advantages. Hopefully, four or five heads are better than one. If the group agrees on a solution, the chances are very good that it will be a quality decision. And perhaps even more important is the fact that the people will probably have a higher degree of acceptance and commitment regarding the decision because it is "ours."

These styles of leadership are very important to consider when making a change. Managers who use the first approach and dictate change and coerce people into implementing it are probably going to meet resentment and resistance. In addition, subordinates have a way of sabotaging decisions that they don't accept. Usually, they are able to do it subtly, and managers often can't figure out why the decision isn't working out very well.

A case in point is the story told by Dave, a manufacturing manager of a well-known Milwaukee manufacturing company. Here is his story:

> I looked over the machines in our plant and selected those that needed to be replaced. The president, manager of engineering, vice-president of finance, and I would select a specific machine to replace. We searched for vendors who manufactured that type of equipment. We checked them out and took the company plane to talk with three or four of

them. We carefully studied each machine and checked with organizations that had purchased them. We would decide which one to buy and would order it. We wanted to surprise the foreman of the department where the new machine would be installed. The foreman first learned of the new machine when it was delivered.

We couldn't figure out why the machine didn't work out as well as we thought it would. It did not improve quality and reduce costs like it had for the other organizations who were using it. It took much more time and maintenance costs to keep it operating effectively. Downtime was much higher than it was for other organizations using the same type of machine.

It finally dawned on us that it wasn't the machine. Rather it had to do with the attitude of the foreman and his employees who were using the machine. It wasn't anything we could put our fingers on. It just seemed they didn't seem to care whether it was working effectively or not. As a matter of fact, we felt that they really didn't want it to work well.

This example from the manufacturing manager may not be too unusual. A person might think that any foreman would like the "surprise" of a brand new machine that would improve quality and cut costs, but resistance to change is often emotional and not factual. In this case, the lack of communication and participation in the decision caused the foreman to have a negative attitude. And his attitude was probably "catching" among his subordinates.

When the manufacturing manager realized what had happened, he changed his approach. In the future, whenever a new machine was being considered, the foreman was immediately involved. When the vendors of the proposed new machine had been identified, the foreman was asked to come along in the company plane to look over the different machines. As a further participatory action, the foreman was asked to select an hourly worker to go along and provide input regarding the decision to purchase. This worker had the qualifications of being a good worker and one who would be working on a new machine.

The decision was made by Maier's second approach described earlier. The final decision was made by the manufacturing manager and other members of top management. But the acceptance level of the foreman and one of his best workers was exceptionally high. They, in turn, influenced the acceptance level of the other workers. Also, the quality of the decision was improved by the input regarding features of the machine that would best fit the needs of the department where it would be installed.

Participation, therefore, is an important ingredient in both the quality and the acceptance of the change. One of the most frequent reasons for resentment and resistance to change is the lack of input by those involved. They frequently feel that they could have contributed *before* the change had been finalized. Their feelings were hurt by higher-level managers who did not ask for their ideas.

Many managers still use the first approach described by Maier and don't ask subordinates for input. Their reason may be pride—they feel that they should know everything and it's a sign of weakness to ask subordinates for ideas. Or, they may feel it is a waste of time—they feel that the contributions from subordinates will not be useful. This may be based on past experience where they have asked and received no worthwhile response. Or, it may be based on the theory "X" philosophy as described by McGregor (1960) in his book, *The Human Side of Enterprise.* Theory "X" managers assume that subordinates don't have ideas that will contribute to the effectiveness of the organization.

When managers realize the importance of participation, the problem becomes one of *when* and *how* to do it.

The "When" of Participation

The following statement offers three alternatives regarding the "when" of asking for participation. Check the blank that indicates your answer.

You have decided to make a radical change in your department:

_____ A. From the beginning, tell your subordinates some of your thoughts including the need for the change and get their reactions and suggestions.

_____ B. Make a "tentative" plan and ask your subordinates for reactions and comments.

_____ C. Prepare a final plan and sell it your subordinates by explaining the need for the change and how you arrive at the final plan.

Answer *A* states that a manager should ask for input even before tentative plans have been made. *B* states that a manager should develop a "tentative" plan and then ask for input. Answer *C* solicits no participation. Either *A* or *B* is the approved answer, with a slight advantage to *A*.

Answer *A* probably gets more input. This input will include ideas as well as feelings of the subordinates. There is no defensiveness on the part of the manager. He or she is open-minded toward all input because no tentative plans have been made. These ideas can be used to develop "tentative" plans that can then be presented to subordinates for more input. As described earlier, this input can improve both quality and acceptance.

A true story illustrates a caution that should be considered if you answered *B*. The president of a large utility called together his top management team and made the following presentation: "If you saw the light in my office until midnight the last two nights, it wasn't the janitor or cleaning lady. I was working on the problem that we've been discussing for the last couple of weeks. I analyzed all the possible causes of the problem. I considered all of the possible solutions. I evaluated each one by analyzing the advantages and disadvantages of each. I've finally selected the best solution. Now I'd like to present it to you as a 'tentative solution' and see what you think of it. Here's my solution."

After presenting the solution, the president asked, "Does anyone have a better solution?"

After a pause in which there were no comments, the president stated, "O.K., we are all agreed. So let's begin immediately to implement the solution."

Out in the hall following the meeting, the following conversation took place between two of the managers who had attended the meeting:

Bill: What do you think of the solution that our president presented?

Tom: I'm not sure.

Bill: What do you mean?

Tom: Well, I have some concerns about the solution. I'm not sure it will work.

Bill: Do you have a suggestion?

Tom: Well, yes—it would be a modification to the solution that was presented.

Bill: Well, why didn't you speak up?

Tom: I'm not that stupid.

What Tom was saying was that the president had presented his solution in such a way that he was obviously not looking for any suggestions. In fact, he would probably have reacted defensively to any suggestion by saying such things as "I considered that when I arrived at my solution," or "Have you given as much thought to your solution as I have to the one I presented?" or "You obviously haven't given it careful attention if you make that kind of a suggestion."

This story illustrates an important caution. When a manager has made a "tentative" plan, he or she is apt to defend it, especially if much time has been spent in preparing the plan. This defensiveness is very apt to discourage subordinates from suggesting modifications or offering negative comments regarding the tentative plan.

In the church reorganization that was described in Chapter Five, participation played an important part. When the decision had been made that some type of reorganization would take place, a task force was established that consisted of two pastors, three deacons, and two members of the congregation. All members of the congregation were apprised of the task force and were asked to give their recommendations to a member. All of these suggestions were considered by the task force when arriving at a decision. Consensus was reached on the new organization structure. This was presented to the board of deacons and then to the congregation. The overwhelming favorable vote by the congregation was influenced by the high degree of participation that had taken place in the decision-making process.

One answer to the "when" of participation then is to get input before the final decision is made. This can be done before and/or after tentative plans have been made. This input can influence the decision itself as well as increase the degree of acceptance of the decision.

Sometimes, however, it is not possible or practical to get input before the decision is made. It, therefore, becomes important to get participation after the decision has been made but before it is implemented. For example, a decision may be made by top management to enrich jobs, as in the following case study.

Case Study

In a company making small radios, the employees worked on an assembly line. One person worked at station 1 and assembled the first part of each radio. This part was passed on to the second station where the second person added to the assembly. This was passed on to the next person and so on until the sixth person assembled the final part. Figure 3(a) shows the present process.

Top management decided that job enrichment of the process would improve quality and quantity of production as well as increase the motivation and job satisfaction of the employees. Figure 3(b) shows the proposed process in which each employee would assemble the entire radio.

In this case, management had made the decision to enrich the jobs without any input from subordinates. Now they must ask for input on how to implement the decision. This can still be very productive for the organization as well as satisfying for the participants.

Figure 3. Radio Job Enrichment Proposal.

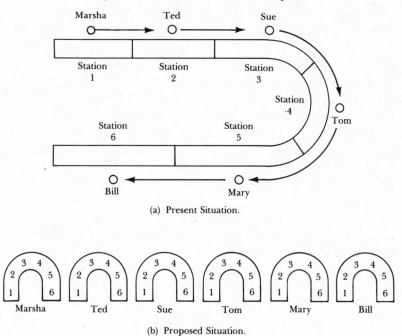

(a) Present Situation.

(b) Proposed Situation.

The "How" of Participation

The most significant aspect of participation is that managers really want the input and are not merely going through the motions of asking for it. They must believe that input will contribute to the effectiveness of the department. The specific steps for getting it include:

1. Ask for input.
2. Seriously consider it and objectively evaluate it.
3. Use those ideas that are good.
4. Reject those that aren't practical.
5. Give credit and other appropriate rewards to those who contributed ideas that were used.
6. Convince those whose ideas were rejected that their ideas were considered, and explain why they were not used.

These steps can be followed on a formal or informal basis. On a formal basis, some examples are quality circles (Mercury Marine), performance circles (Dorsey Trailers), correction action teams (IBM), positive action teams (Honeywell), participative management program (Motorola), pride teams (Data General), people councils (Pontiac Motor Division of General Motors), and participation groups (Fleetwood Plant of General Motors.) All of these programs ask employees to volunteer to be part of a circle or team to improve the efficiency and effectiveness of the department in which they work. Groups vary in size from three to ten people. Usually, they spend one hour a week on company time to identify problems, arrive at solutions, and make recommendations to higher management. Sometimes the supervisor is the leader and sometimes one of the workers is selected as the leader. The leaders and members of the circles are trained in problem-solving techniques. They work together to arrive at the best solution. Approximately 95 percent of their recommendations are approved by higher management. The rewards to the participants include personal satisfaction, job security, and recognition. Rarely do companies give them financial rewards for their input.

Informal approaches are used by other organizations. Sometimes, it takes the form of problem-solving meetings in which employees are asked for their ideas in group meetings. These meetings are usually called as needed instead of being scheduled on a one-hour-a-week basis. The participants have no training in problem solving. The manager conducts the meeting and strives to get the group to reach a consensus on the best solution. The size of groups varies from three to eight or more people who have been selected by the manager.

Another informal approach is for managers to provide a job climate in which subordinates are encouraged to offer suggestions at any time. Or, managers may ask one or more individuals for input on a particular problem whenever they feel the input will be helpful.

Regardless of the approach, it is necessary to follow the six specific steps just described. It is especially important to maintain the enthusiasm of those whose ideas were not used. This can be done by convincing them that their ideas were carefully considered. They must also be sold on the reasons why their ideas were not used. Otherwise, their desire to offer future suggestions will be greatly diminished.

In the radio job enrichment case described earlier in this chapter, input from subordinates can be solicited in two different ways: (1) asking for ideas for implementing the change from the present assembly line process to the new approach, and (2) training the other employees to learn the new job. A group meeting, for example, would be called to communicate the decision to change and ask for ideas on how to implement it. Some of the ideas would probably be:

- "Let those who want to change do it while those who don't want to do it keep doing it the old way."
- "Let those who want to go from one process to all six do it. Let the rest go from one to two or to three, or to whatever number of jobs they think they can handle."
- "Instead of jumping from one task to six, go from one to three and try that for a while. Then add one more task as skill and confidence are developed."
- "Let those who are doing each job train the others."

Each idea would be considered and the manager would use either Maier's second approach (ask for input but make the decision himself/herself) or the third approach (arrive at group consensus). The manager should decide which approach to use before the meeting and let the group know at the start.

Cautions to Consider

Participative management is not a panacea for solving all problems and making everybody happy. Kanter (1983) with tongue in cheek coined the following phrase: "Participation is something the top orders the middle to do for the bottom." This approach, of course, is bound to fail. It must start with the top believing that participation is important and practicing it at their level. As Emerson once said, "What you do thunders so loudly I can't hear what you say."

Participation needs to be managed just as carefully as any other system because it will probably create some problems by solving others. For example, some managers won't accept the fact that it is good. They may give it lip service and go through the motions but won't do it enthusiastically. Top management must be aware of this and be prepared to take appropriate action. At the new Nissan light truck plant in Tennessee, for example, top management clearly states that they will get rid of any manager who doesn't believe and practice the company philosophy of participative management. This becomes an important criterion in both selection and promotion.

Another problem involves employees who are very skeptical of the whole process. They don't believe that management is really concerned about their quality of work life (QWL). They feel that management wants to get their ideas without providing any reward. In fact, they are afraid their ideas might backfire by improving productivity and reducing the number of employees. The reward for a good dollar-saving idea might be termination. This attitude may be particularly common where unions have a "them versus us" feeling toward management. It might also be true in organizations in which managers have never asked for or listened to the input of employees. This has been particularly true in the automobile industry where there has been a lack of rapport between managers and workers. It will take time and patience to solve this problem. Action in addition to words will have to convince employees that participation is a new way of life. A foundation of mutual respect, cooperation, and open communication is needed.

The question of whether participation should be voluntary or mandatory must be carefully considered. People vary in their desire to participate. In most organizations with formal programs, participation is voluntary. However, there may be a stigma attached to a person who does not decide to "volunteer." Peer pressure may also be involved. Whatever the approach, managers should be constantly alert for negative attitudes toward participation and handle each situation on an individual basis.

Leadership is also an important consideration. In most organizations a formal leader is selected. In some companies the leader of quality circles and other formal groups is the supervisor. In other organizations it is a worker selected by the rest of the group. Either situation can succeed or fail, depending on the attitude and skills of the leader. Organizations should be sure that the best person is selected and trained to provide the leadership to make the group effective.

An important caution has to do with the speed with which participative programs are implemented. Many quality circle programs have failed because an organization has tried to move too fast. The proper approach consists of the following steps:

1. Select a steering committee that establishes policies and procedures.
2. Select a facilitator who will be responsible for planning and implementing a program.
3. Train the facilitator in philosophy, procedures, forms, and techniques.
4. Start with one or two pilot groups.
5. Provide training for the leader and group members.
6. Move slowly in establishing new circles.

The best advice is to move slowly and steadily, rather than try to establish too many circles at once. One other caution is to be sure that the facilitator is provided with the time and resources to manage the program successfully. Some organizations have picked a person to be facilitator who still has too many other tasks to perform.

According to Kanter (1983, pp. 275-276), there is a need for participation to be well managed and balanced:

> Well-managed systems have these elements: a clearly designed management structure and involvement of the appropriate line people; assignment of meaningful and manageable tasks with clear boundaries and parameters; a time frame, a set of accountability and reporting relationships, and standards that groups must meet; information and training for participants to help them make participation work effectively; a mechanism for involving all of those with a

stake in the issue, to avoid the problems of power and to ensure for those who have input or interest a chance to get involved; a mechanism for providing visibility, recognition, and rewards for teams' efforts; and clearly understood processes for the formation of participative groups, their ending, and the transfer of the learning from them.

It is clear that managing participation is a balancing act between management control and team opportunity, between getting the work done quickly and giving people a chance to learn, between seeking volunteers and pushing people into it, and between too little team spirit and too much.

But the long-term impact of well-managed participatory vehicles for energizing the grass roots and involving them in innovation should be a more adaptive organization, one that can more easily live with, and even stay ahead of, change. It is not so much that employee motivation will be improved as that the organization may be better able to tap and take advantage of employee ideas. Employees, in turn, may be more adaptable—more skilled and thus more flexible, more able to move with changes, and more favorably disposed toward management initiatives for change in which they know they can play a role.

Summary

Participation is a very important factor in the successful management of change. It begins with a philosophy among all levels of management beginning at the top. They must believe that participation can benefit both the organization and the employees.

It then requires implementation. In most cases a formal approach is best. This would include a specific program such as quality circles with its structure and training. In some cases an informal approach can be successful.

Not only can participation contribute to the quality of the change, but it can also be significant in increasing the acceptance of those who must implement the change. And this is what "managing" change is all about. It involves both the decision itself and its implementation. A "good" decision based

on all of the available facts can fail because of lack of acceptance resulting in resistance and even sabotage. Participation is
the key that can contribute to both quality and acceptance and
result in a win/win solution for both manager and subordinates.
One organization called their program PI/PS, which stands for
productivity improvement/personal satisfaction. Both can be
accomplished through an effective participation program.

9

CICICICICICICICICICICICICICICICICICICICICICIC

Applying the Three Keys

The three keys, empathy, communication, and participation, have been defined in the last three chapters. They are illustrated in the following case studies in which I was personally involved.

Developing and Implementing a New Performance Appraisal Program
International Minerals and Chemical Corporation (IMC)
Skokie, Illinois

When I joined IMC, my first assignment was to develop a new performance appraisal program. My plan was to develop a program, sell it to my boss (director of industrial relations), and have it adopted as a corporate program to be implemented in all divisions of IMC. To develop the program, I read books, attended seminars, visited other organizations, and studied the approaches being used by the various departments within IMC.

The plan that I developed was to be implemented by all managers with their salaried employees on an annual basis. The major objective of the program was for each manager to work with his or her subordinates to help them improve their performance. A secondary objective was to provide performance information that would be useful for personnel actions including salary increases, transfers, and promotions.

The performance appraisal and review program consisted of the following steps:

1. The manager and subordinate would jointly agree on the major segments of the subordinate's job.

151

2. The manager and subordinate would jointly establish "standards of performance."
3. The manager would appraise the performance of the subordinate in relation to the standards.
4. The subordinate would appraise his or her performance in relation to the standards.
5. The manager would conduct a performance appraisal interview to agree on a fair appraisal and determine strengths and weaknesses of the subordinate.
6. The manager and subordinate would jointly develop a performance improvement plan for one area of performance needing improvement.
7. The manager would coach the subordinate in implementing the performance improvement plan.

This approach was not only very different than any previous IMC program but it was also more complicated and would require more of the manager's time. We realized that most managers would probably resist it unless they were convinced that the resulting improved performance and better relationships with subordinates were worth the time and energy needed to implement the program. Many IMC managers had been exposed to some type of performance appraisal program that hadn't been helpful to them. Therefore, in order to get the managers to accept and hopefully welcome the program, we realized that three things had to be done:

1. We had to *communicate* so that managers would understand the objectives and various steps of the program. They must realize that it was a tool to help them manage and not a personnel department program.
2. We had to *sell* the program so that managers would feel that it was worth the time and energy required of them.
3. We had to *provide training* so that managers would have the necessary knowledge and skills to implement the program.

We finalized the program and were ready to communicate and sell it to higher-level corporate management when I got a call from Jack Devlin, director of industrial relations at our Carlsbad, New Mexico, mining division. He had learned of our program and asked me to come to Carlsbad to explain the program to see if they wanted to implement it.

So I went to Carlsbad and described the program to him, the general manager, and the management development supervisor. With minor modifications, they accepted the program and asked me to help them implement it. We discussed the best approach and agreed on the following:

1. I would communicate the program to the eight major department heads who reported to the general manager.
2. They would in turn communicate the proposed program to the supervisors who reported to them.
3. At a dinner meeting of all salaried employees, the general manager would announce the program and explain that I had been invited to help them implement the program. I would then communicate the program.
4. I would train the thirty-five managers who would conduct appraisal interviews with their subordinates.
5. The management development supervisor at Carlsbad would coordinate the program.

Everything proceeded as planned. All except one of the general manager's subordinates were enthusiastic about the program. The mining superintendent didn't like the paperwork that was involved but agreed to go along with it. The date of the dinner meeting was set and announced.

At the dinner, the general manager explained that his management team had decided to implement the program. He made it clear that it was not imposed by the home office at Skokie. He introduced me as the person who had developed the program and would help with its implementation. He mentioned that it would be coordinated by the Carlsbad management development supervisor.

I communicated and sold the program with the help of a pamphlet that described the program and a set of slides. Following the presentation, I answered questions.

The next step was to train the managers. The thirty-five managers were divided into groups of seventeen and eighteen and training meetings were held to develop skills and knowledge in the following steps of the performance appraisal program.

1. How to determine significant job segments.
2. How to develop standards of performance.
3. How to appraise performance.
4. How to conduct the appraisal interview.
5. How to develop the performance improvement plan.
6. How to coach subordinates.

In each meeting, discussion was held, assignments were given, and skills were developed.

In coordinating the program, the management development supervisor prepared the proper forms, established performance interview schedules, and provided help where needed. Each month, the general manager was given a report of interviews scheduled and conducted. Where interviews were not conducted as scheduled, he talked with the appropriate managers and saw to it that the interviews were held.

In summary, the success of the program was achieved because of the following factors:

- The careful development of the program.
- The input and approval by the three key people at Carlsbad. They considered it their program and not one imposed by the corporate office.
- The special efforts to communicate to everyone concerned, beginning with top management.
- The selling of the program to all employees on the basis of the benefits.
- The training to teach the necessary knowledge and skills.
- The coordination by the management development supervisor.
- The active support of the general manager.

The decision to install the program was made by local management and not imposed by the corporate office. It was *their* program and the corporate office provided the necessary assistance. Also, line management made the decision to implement the program. The personnel department provided the staff assistance. This participation in both the decision and implementation was a major factor in its success.

Empathy, the first key, was used to determine the possible reaction to a new, relatively complicated program. We realized that some resistance would be present because of past experience and also because it would take quite a bit of time to complete the forms, conduct the interviews, and work out plans for improvement. We felt that both communication and participation would be needed to overcome the potential resistance.

The communication process was carefully planned. The program was explained to the three key persons, the top management staff of eight managers, the other supervisors, and finally all employees who would be involved. Visual aids were used and questions were encouraged. Benefits as well as forms and procedures were carefully explained.

As far as participation was concerned, the original program was developed after getting input from the people at IMC who had experience with performance appraisals. Next, the input came from the three key managers at Carlsbad who suggested minor changes to the program as originally planned. The third attempt at participation was to get the eight upper-level managers to offer their reactions and suggestions to the proposed program. The input of the thirty-five managers was also an important part of the training program.

The philosophy, principles, and procedures of this program became the basis for the book, *How to Improve Performance Through Appraisal and Coaching* (Kirkpatrick, 1982).

Developing and Implementing a Program for
Selecting Foremen
Bendix Products Aerospace Division
South Bend, Indiana

Soon after I assumed my position as personnel manager of Bendix Products Aerospace Division, Dick Whiffen, the general manager, called me into his office. The following conversation took place:

Dick: I'm not satisfied with the way in which our foremen have been selected.

Don: Tell me more.

Dick: From what I can understand, emphasis has been placed on their performance as "doers" and also on their seniority. And I don't think these are the most important criteria for promoting a worker to foreman.

Don: What do you suggest?

Dick: I'm going to give you a special assignment, in addition to your regular job, of course.

Don: What kind of assignment?

Dick: I'm going to charge you with the job of seeing to it that we do a better job of picking foremen in the future.

Don: What do you want me to do?

Dick: You tell me. You are supposed to be an expert in selection, aren't you?

Don: I guess so.

Dick: Well, I leave it up to you to come to me with some recommendations.

Don: Will you do me a favor?

Dick: What kind of favor?

Don: Will you please tell Tim, the manufacturing manager, what you told me. He may not like me telling him how to pick "his" foremen.

Dick: O.K. I'll tell him.

This was the beginning of a major change in the approach to selecting future foremen.

The first step was for Dick, Tim, and myself to get together to discuss past practice and the problems it caused. Tim agreed that two common faults existed: (1) In some cases, we picked a poor foreman and lost an excellent worker, and (2) in many cases, a worker was told on a Friday that he would be a foreman on Monday, and no orientation or training was provided. We agreed that I would develop a tentative approach and discuss it with Dick and Tim.

After I presented a tentative plan and we discussed it, the three of us agreed on the following approach:

1. We would select a "pool" of potential foremen. The "pool" would contain approximately twice as many people as would be promoted to the position of foreman during the next year.
2. In selecting people for the "pool," the first criterion would be the desire of the worker to be a foreman.
3. Other criteria to be considered would be:
    * Past performance.
    * Attitude.
    * Technical knowledge.
    * Age (forty-five or under).
    * Intelligence (minimum score of twenty-four on Wonderlic "Personnel Test."
    * Education (high school required).
    It should be noted that at the time this program was developed, factors such as age, intelligence, and education were considered acceptable criteria.
4. When workers had been selected for the pool, they would be required to attend an eighteen-hour presupervisory training program on their own time. Subjects would include leadership, communication, labor relations, training, and discipline.
5. When an opening occurred, line management would review data and pick the person for the job.
6. Future foremen would be picked from the pool. Any exceptions would have to be approved by the general manager.
7. Candidates who were not selected for the pool would be so notified.

Obviously, this procedure was a major change from the simple process that had been used. In the past, the general foreman, superintendent, and/or manufacturing manager simply picked the person because of good performance, much seniority, and a cooperative attitude. In many cases, they talked the reluctant worker into accepting the job with the promise that "we'll help you get started and we'll help you when you have problems."

The first question we considered in making this change was, "How will people react to the change?" The obvious answer was some people would favor it and others would not like it. For example, when Dick told me of the new assignment, I anticipated that Tim would not like me, the new personnel manager, telling him whom to promote. Therefore, I asked Dick to tell him that my job as a staff person was to help him. We were all interested in the same objective—to pick the best foremen—and I emphasized that the best job would be done if we worked together. I also emphasized that the final decision in picking a foreman would be made by line management, with my help if requested.

We also anticipated that general foremen and superintendents might not appreciate help from the personnel department in decisions that they had previously made. So we presented our plan to these people as well as to the present foremen, to be sure they understood the why, what, and how of the change. In one of the meetings, a general foreman asked the question "What happens if the worker I think would be the best foreman doesn't volunteer for the program?" The answer was, "Then he couldn't be picked. If you know of such a person, be sure to encourage him to apply for the program."

Another source of possible resistance was the union. We told the union leaders what we were going to do. Fortunately, they didn't seem to care. It didn't seem to make any difference to them how workers were picked for the job of foreman.

We figured that some workers would like the idea, some would oppose it, and most would be neutral because they probably weren't interested in becoming a foreman anyway. But we wanted all of them to be apprised of what we were doing.

Our first step in communicating to the 2,000 hourly employees was to announce it in our monthly newsletter, the *Aerospacer*. The next step was to send a letter from the general manager to the home of each factory worker, as shown in Exhibit 4. Those who were interested completed the form shown in Exhibit 5. Of the 2,000 employees, 130 returned the completed form and 93 showed up for the testing.

Part of the screening process was to evaluate their job performance, particularly as it related to aspects of leadership that

Exhibit 4. Foreman Selection Letter.

THE BENDIX CORPORATION
Bendix Products Aerospace Division • South Bend 20, Indiana

TO: Aerospace Hourly Employees

SUBJECT: Preforeman Training Program

As mentioned in my recent letter we are now ready to offer preforemen training to our employees. This is a program whereby we want to select and train employees who have the potential to become foremen. Then, when new jobs open up, we will fill them from this group. We believe in promotion from within, and are going to try this program as a way of putting into practice what we believe. Here is our program:

1. All candidates will be carefully screened to determine those we feel have the best potential for the job.
   a. The candidate will be given three paper and pencil tests to give us an indication of mental ability, mechanical aptitude, and knowledge of supervisory principles.
   b. We will get a performance appraisal from foremen who have supervised the candidate.
   c. If advisable, the candidate may be given a medical exam.
2. Candidates will be selected by the general manager, manufacturing manager and the personnel manager.
3. A training program will be given on the candidate's own time. It will include such subjects as:
   a. The Foreman's Job
   b. Planning & Organizing Work
   c. Understanding & Motivating People
   d. Training Subordinates
   e. Labor Relations
   f. Communications
   g. Aerospace Division Policies & Procedures
4. Graduates of the program will be considered for such positions as openings occur.

Please understand that candidates for this program will be selected on the basis of their potential to become foremen. If you are selected for the training program, we cannot guarantee you a foreman's job after successful completion of the course; however, your chances of being chosen for the position will be greatly enhanced.

We feel that there are many people interested in improving themselves. They will want to complete the enclosed application and return it to Don Kirkpatrick, our Personnel Manager. Your application will be kept in strict confidence. Your applications must be received by December 13 to be considered.

If you have further questions, please contact Don directly.

Sincerely,

R. E. Whiffen
General Manager

P.S. Even though the program is designed to select and train future foremen, some of the candidates may be offered other salary jobs in manufacturing, quality control and production control.

Exhibit 5. Application Blank for Preforeman Training Program.

Bendix Products Aerospace Division

1. Name _____ Dept. _____

2. Street Address _____ City _____ Phone _____

3. Date of Birth _____ Date Employed by Bendix _____

4. Jobs Held at Bendix _____

   _____

   _____

5. Jobs Held at Other Companies _____

   _____

6. Education
   a. Please circle last grade completed:
      1 2 3 4 5 6 7 8 9 10 11 12   1 2 3 4
          Grade and High School   College
   b. List any special courses you have taken (night school, correspon-
      dence, vocational school, etc.)
      Name of Course _____ School _____ Yr. _____
      Name of Course _____ School _____ Yr. _____
      Name of Course _____ School _____ Yr. _____
   c. Other comments on education_____

      _____

7. Leadership Activities (List any offices held and other leadership activities)

   _____

   _____

   _____

8. Other information that might be important in considering you for a
   foreman's job.

   _____

   _____

I understand that this application will be held in strict confidence. I also
understand that there is no guarantee that I will become a foreman even if
I complete the training.

_____   _____
        DATE   SIGNATURE

would be important in a foreman's job. The form shown in Exhibit 6 was completed by each foreman who had supervised the worker. This input from foreman was an important factor in the success of the program.

Based on an analysis of all the available data, Dick, Tim and I selected twenty-three people for the pool. Of these, we predicted that approximately twelve would be promoted during the next year.

An important aspect of the program was communication with all the candidates. Table 1 shows the various steps that were used.

This program was a dramatic change in the process of picking foremen. It turned out to be a most successful program. Feedback from everyone concerned was positive. A similar approach was used in a number of organizations that learned about the program. The keys to the success of the program were empathy, communication, and participation.

A detailed description of this Bendix case plus similar case studies from Inland Steel Company and Kearney & Trecker Corporation are described in the 325-page manual, *How to Select and Train New First-Line Supervisors* (Kirkpatrick, Coverdale, and Olsen-Tjensvold, 1980).

Making Changes Successfully

There are many reasons why changes work out or don't. Some of the factors are past experience with change, the general morale of the organization, attitudes of upper management, and economic conditions. But the bottom line is whether or not good decisions are made and whether or not these decisions are accepted by the people who must implement them. Poor decisions to change, even if implemented successfully, are going to have bad results. Likewise, good decisions that are not accepted by those involved are not going to be successful.

Whenever a decision is considered, empathy should be used to try to determine how people will react to the change. In the film called "Overcoming Resistance to Change," Keith, the manager states, "When we decided to make this change in equipment, I was in favor of the change and I thought all my

Exhibit 6. Performance Appraisal Form.

Name of Candidate _____

Length of Time Under My Supervision   Years _____ Months _____

1. Job Performance?
   ☐ Very good   ☐ Satisfactory   ☐ Unsatisfactory

2. Supervision Required?
   ☐ A great deal   ☐ Average   ☐ Very little

3. Attitude toward management?
   ☐ Very good   ☐ Average   ☐ Negative

4. How well get along with others?
   ☐ Very well   ☐ Average   ☐ Poorly

5. Does he/she create problems for supervision?   ☐ Yes   ☐ No
   If yes, explain _____
   _____
   _____

6. Absence   ☐ Never   ☐ Occasional   ☐ Frequent
   Tardiness   ☐ Never   ☐ Occasional   ☐ Frequent
   Health   ☐ Never   ☐ Occasional   ☐ Frequent
   Comments: _____
   _____
   _____

7. Do you have any evidence that this person has leadership ability? (on the job or outside evidence)
   ☐ Yes   ☐ No   If yes, give details _____
   _____
   _____
   _____

8. How would he/she be in regard to the following items:

Yes	No		Yes	No	
____	____	Would be a good communicator	____	____	Would accept responsibility
____	____	Would be too bossy	____	____	Good organizer
____	____	Would be easily influenced by employees	____	____	Would stand up for subordinates
____	____	Would be a "Yes" person	____	____	Would give credit
____	____	Would be overly concerned with details	____	____	Would be loyal to company
____	____	Would be a good trainer	____	____	Would be helpful to employee having a problem

Exhibit 6. Performance Appraisal Form, Cont'd.

Yes	No		Yes	No	
___	___	Would give instruc-structions clearly	___	___	Would be capable in handling grievances
___	___	Would be a "buck passer"	___	___	Would let employees know where they stand
___	___	Would be cost conscious			
___	___	Would be able to influence his/her boss	___	___	Would be likely to show favoritism
___	___	Would be well liked by subordinates	___	___	Would have respect of subordinates

9. To what extent would you recommend this person as a foreperson?

   ☐ Strongly recommend   ☐ Mildly recommend

   ☐ Do not recommend   ☐ Uncertain

   Additional factors (favorable or not) that should be considered:

   _____

   _____

   _____   _____
   Date   Signature of Foreman

   _____   _____
   Date   Signature of General Foreman

NOTE: The signature of the General Foreman doesn't necessarily mean agreement with the appraisal by the foreman. It simply means that he has seen it.

people were also in favor of the change." As the film progressed, he realized that the poor results of the change were due to lack of acceptance and not to the decision. He finally learned how his subordinates felt and why they resisted the change. With this knowledge, he was able to proceed and get the acceptance of each one.

The need for communication is obvious. All those who are involved need to understand the change and the reasons for it. And the communication should go down through channels to

Table 1. Communicating with Candidates for Foreman.

Situa-tion	When	How	To Whom
1.	After all applications for the program have been received (cut-off date)	Letter from person who received applications acknowledging receipt, and outlining selection process	All applicants
2.	Seven days prior to the date set for any step in the process	Notices reminding candidate of event, when, where, and so on	All applicants remaining in process
3.	Immediately following a candidate's failure to appear or qualify in a step in the process	Letter confirming the applicant's failure to appear or to qualify and informing him/her of a make-up date, if any, or dropping him/her from further consideration	All candidates who do not complete all steps of the selection process
4.	Immediately after completion of the selection process	Letter confirming the candidate's completion of the process and informing him/her how and when final selection will be made	All remaining candidates
5.	When selection is made	Letter to successful candidates informing them of their selection	All those selected
6.	When selection is made	Letter to unsuccessful candidates notifying them of who was selected and what they can do to prepare for the next opportunity. Also, information on whom they can talk with to find out why they weren't selected	All those rejected

be sure that each manager understands the change before his or her subordinates do. This is very important, primarily because feelings and emotions are involved. Also, opportunities must be given to ask questions and the questions must be answered. The "fear of the unknown" should be eliminated whenever possible.

More and more organizations are recognizing the need for participation in order to get changes accepted, not only initially but on a long-range basis. It is widely recognized by authors and managers alike that people who have provided input into a decision are more likely to accept and be committed to it. And commitment to change is an important goal to achieve. In addition, input from those involved can provide ideas that can help managers arrive at higher-quality decisions. Quality and acceptance of decisions are both important to the success of a change.

It's time for a change. It may be small or it may be large. It may come down from higher management, it may be suggested by subordinates or peers, or managers may think of themselves, but it is present. To be effective, managers must recognize that it is a way of life. The key to their success is their ability to manage it so that the best decisions are made with the highest level of acceptance by those who must implement them.

Part III

ⵔⵔⵔⵔⵔⵔⵔⵔⵔⵔⵔⵔⵔⵔⵔⵔⵔⵔⵔⵔⵔⵔⵔⵔⵔⵔⵔ

Case Examples of Successful Change

ⵔⵔⵔⵔⵔⵔⵔⵔⵔⵔⵔⵔⵔⵔⵔⵔⵔⵔⵔⵔⵔⵔⵔⵔⵔⵔⵔ

This part of *How to Manage Change Effectively* contains case studies that illustrate how changes can be decided on and implemented successfully in various sizes and types of organizations. The following brief summaries will help the reader decide which cases will be most pertinent to his or her needs. The reader will want to take particular note of the philosophy, principles, and methods that are illustrated in each case. Many of these can be applied in similar organizations and situations.

Chapter Ten considers the problems faced by employees who are promoted to managerial positions. In striving to be successful in their new roles, such employees must decide how fast to move in making changes. The challenge is the same whether one is promoted from within or hired from the outside. In this case study from the military, Peter Land (1983) describes what he did to be effective in his new job. His philosophy and approach have general applications in all types and sizes of organizations.

Changes in personnel policy are common in industry, business, and government. Chapter Eleven describes how at Northwestern Mutual Life Insurance Company, the change to variable working hours was carefully planned and implemented, resulting in a high acceptance level among managers as well as employees. A careful study of this case will provide guidelines for personnel policy changes in any organization.

Nearly every organization is interested in reducing costs while improving productivity. In Chapter Twelve, consultant Roy Walters describes his philosophy of work design, known as work effectiveness, and how it was successfully applied at Citibank to improve productivity and decrease costs. The principles can be applied in nearly every organization.

More and more organizations are adopting a strong philosophy of participative management because they realize its potential benefit both to the organization and to the individual. Chapter Thirteen describes the implementing of quality circles, the most common application of participative management. In writing the chapter, Sud Ingle uses examples from Mercury Marine, a manufacturing organization, and a hospital. Some do's and don't's are included to describe how a quality circle program can be successful.

In Chapter Fourteen, authors Blake and Mouton use a case study to illustrate how behavior norms of both managers and nonmanagers can be changed in order to improve productivity and still maintain high morale. The case titled "Getting More Productivity from the Last Hour of Work," demonstrates the need for active participation by those involved. It describes how a group of supervisors reach agreement on the need for a change and how it is effectively implemented.

In manufacturing organizations, an incentive system often determines the pay of the workers. Changing such a system is strongly resisted by workers if they feel they will lose money or security. Chapter Fifteen describes a company with a philosophy of concern for its employees. It demonstrates how this philosophy was the basis for a carefully planned change that was implemented with a high degree of acceptance on the part of management and workers.

Manufacturing managers will recognize the significance of the case study in Chapter Sixteen, which describes switching from a "batch" to a "just-in-time" process—a major change. The

IBM operation at Rochester, Minnesota, borrowed the "just-in-time" idea from Japan and adapted it to a complicated process. By communicating clearly and obtaining input from those involved, the system was successfully changed, with improved productivity and lower cost.

Reorganizing in order to accomplish objectives is always a challenge. Even after the decision has been made, it is often difficult to get it accepted. In the case study, in Chapter Seventeen, Xerox decided to integrate its sales forces so that its sales personnel would handle a variety of products. Careful planning, complete communication, and extensive involvement allowed the change to be successfully implemented.

Hospitals have not been leaders in the training and development of managers. Typically, the nursing department has been responsible for its own training while the other managers may not have had any organized training at all. Chapter Eighteen describes how a full-blown training department was planned and implemented in a hospital. One of the big challenges was to centralize all management training, including nursing personnel. Empathy, communication, and participation were all present in this successful change.

10

Moving into a
New Managerial Job

When a person moves into a new managerial job, he or she must decide how to proceed. Making changes becomes a very delicate matter. The following case study describes the success of an air force colonel who took over a new command. He describes the philosophy and approaches that made him successful. He found that it was important to "know the territory" and gain the respect of subordinates. He established an open-door policy for informal discussions. He encouraged subordinates to make their own decisions. He used praise and other forms of positive reinforcement for good work. He created a climate for teamwork through communication and participation.

The philosophy and principles described by Peter Land would apply in almost every situation where a person moves into a management job.

"Sir, I Assume Command"
Colonel Peter A. Land, USAF (Ret.)
Montgomery, Alabama

With those words of the title and an exchange of salutes, I began the most challenging, frustrating, rewarding, satisfying, aggravating, broadening, and time-consuming job of my Air Force career. As base commander of Scott AFB, Illinois, I was at the helm of the 375th Air Base Group—1,500 military and civilian personnel. I was charged with the responsibility of operating and maintaining an installation with physical assets valued at more than $615 million and of supporting some 22,000 people who lived, worked, and played there. We supported Hq Military Airlift Command (MAC) and Hq Air Force Communications Command with fifteen general officers residing on base.

As base commander, I learned a number of lessons, some of which may prove useful to others assuming command of a major organization. I would like to discuss how one gets up to speed quickly in such a job, and share some thoughts on my philosophy of command.

How does a person who has never commanded anything assume such a position only three days after arrival on base? There is no formal break-in period; the full responsibilities transfer to you on the effective date of the assumption of command orders. However, from a practical standpoint there is a brief honeymoon period when your boss and subordinates and the public expect you to "learn the territory." Unfortunately, from the outset, you are under close scrutiny by everyone. The people have a natural expectation that the "new kid on the block" will do something positive relatively soon to improve the organization. I have found that several new commanders fell into this trap because of the pressure to "take command and do something spectacular." My challenge was simply—"How do I learn the job quickly and create a positive impression on my people without doing something dumb on day one?"

Note: This article is reprinted from Air University Review, 1983, 34 (6), 20–28. Used by permission.

One advantage I had was having spent three years as the Director of Management Consultation at the Leadership and Management Development Center, Maxwell Air Force Base, Alabama. In that capacity, I worked closely with many senior commanders in diagnosing and solving organizational problems; therefore, I had a feel for the role of a base commander. However, there were some preparatory actions I took which may be useful if you are scheduled to take command without the luxury of having served as a deputy or vice commander.

Before departing Maxwell AFB en route to Scott AFB, I visited with the Maxwell base commander. I attended his staff meetings, shadowed him for a few afternoons, and made orientation visits to each of the major functional areas under his supervision: Civil Engineering, Personnel, Security Police, Disaster Preparedness, etc. I also chatted with a few Air War College and Air Command and Staff College students who had recently completed tours at Scott AFB.

The Base Commander's Management Course (BCMC) is a four-week program designed to prepare prospective base commanders and deputy base commanders for their jobs. Since it is taught at Maxwell, I managed to attend a few classes and scrounged copies of their handouts which gave detailed information on the various functions of air base groups and combat support groups. Many evenings were spent studying the BCMC information. When questions developed, I called the local base functional expert for clarification.

I contacted the Scott AFB Public Affairs Office and requested several back issues of the base newspaper and asked them to send a copy each week until I moved to Scott. One can learn much about a base by studying the base newspaper in detail. The point is that considerable information may be available at your present base pertaining to a command position you are scheduled to assume.

During the three-day overlap with the incumbent, he offered candid views of the strengths and weaknesses of the organization. He introduced me to my new boss, my deputy and staff, as well as selected key people, including certain civilian dignitaries. In the evenings I read recent correspondence files and reviewed the base and wing regulations and operating instructions. I took driving tours of the base with a map in order to become familiar with major facilities, street names, and key areas.

After the change of command ceremony, I met with the command section—deputy, executive officer, and our two secretaries. I stressed that the deputy would be advising me heavily, and they could expect me to follow his advice in most cases. I think it is important to develop a close team spirit among the staff in your immediate office complex—good, open communications and trust are essential elements of command.

That same evening I had dinner with my boss, the wing commander. I asked what he expected from me and my organization, what was important, what issues were politically sensitive, etc. It is absolutely essential to get all the cards on the table as soon as possible—'tis far better than finding the jokers the hard way.

Within a few days I had appointments to pay courtesy calls on each general officer on base. The thrust of my remarks was mainly social, but I asked, "What can the base do to serve you and your organization better?" They seemed to appreciate an active willingness to serve and listen, and my visits also established good rapport that proved later to be invaluable when problems and sensitive issues were raised.

Perhaps the toughest aspect of commanding an organization with which you have had little experience is becoming technically knowledgeable and competent to discuss issues or make decisions. Hq Military Airlift Command has a Commander's Orientation Program that includes briefings not only from each functional directorate and an assessment of its function on Scott AFB but on MAC policy as well. These briefings are very helpful in providing background on certain critical issues.

Next was a formal introduction to the Air Base Group. The functional orientation used was taken, in part, from a command transition model used in the U.S. Army. I adapted it to my situation. For sake of simplicity, I will discuss the Civil Engineering orientation as an example of how I approached every function under my supervision. The first step was to study recent management effectiveness inspection and staff assistance visit reports concerning civil engineering. I also reviewed my notes from my orientation briefing presented by Hq MAC Civil Engineering.

The next step was to obtain an organizational-functional chart of Civil Engineering, including the names of key personnel. I asked the base civil engineer to get his staff together and prepare a formal in-brief to be presented in his conference room with key staff present. I stressed that they cover any subject they felt appropriate, but I wanted the following topics addressed as a minimum:

- mission,
- concept of operation,
- manning situation,
- financial status,
- main customer population,
- feedback systems from customer population,
- greatest challenges,
- goals and objectives,
- major achievements,
- key coordinating units,
- training program, and
- base commander's role.

I have found that when a staff discusses its mission, goals, objectives, etc., teamwork and communications tend to improve. Perhaps the greatest benefit of my orientation was realized in the unit during the preparation for my visit—that was one of my main objectives.

Suppose we look briefly at each of these topics to see why they were selected.

- *Mission.* Reviewing the mission statement reinforces a unit's purpose and gives meaningfulness to the efforts of all assigned personnel. When discussing the unit's mission, I also stressed that we have an implied mission to develop our people professionally while accomplishing the stated mission.
- *Concept of operation.* I wanted an overview of how the unit

performed its mission; this helped me to see the "how" of an organization. I was looking for broad processes, not detailed procedures.

- *Manning status.* In addition to learning the total numbers of authorized as opposed to assigned personnel, we were equally concerned with grade structure, skill levels, and overall experience and quality of supervision. These were key factors in determining a unit's organizational maturity.

- *Financial status.* A few pointed questions can disclose what active controls are established to track and reduce costs. What are the valued incentives to demonstrate skilled financial management at unit level?

- *Main customer population.* If a unit is in the support business, such as an air base group, determining the major users of a particular service being provided is helpful. For example, the base chapel serves the entire family, with the majority of its flock coming from families quartered on base.

- *Feedback systems.* "What systems or procedures are there to learn from your main customer population whether they feel you are meeting their needs?" On occasion, a staff assistance visit may result in praise of your housekeeping and paperwork. But the key question is, "Are you actually accomplishing your service mission?" A feedback system will help you answer that question.

- *Greatest challenges.* "What does the corporate body see as the greatest challenges of the next six-twelve months?" Developing this phase of the briefing period set standards of excellence and improved teamwork. This is the platform on which action plans are built.

- *Goals and objectives.* This is similar to challenges except that goals are more positive and tend to stimulate creativity. People tend to set goals for themselves that are more ambitious than those imposed from above.

- *Major achievements.* Citing major achievements stimulates pride if the record has been good or fosters humility if there is not much to boast about. (I make mental notes to comment on as I visit the individual in his work area.)

- *Key coordinating units.* The commander has a special responsibility to ensure there is a positive relationship between key coordinating units. For example, the interaction between the legal office and the security police is critical to the administration of discipline. On occasion, the nonverbal cues can suggest problems when an organization describes its key coordinating units. That is one area to fix quickly—teamwork and mutual support are essential.

- *Training program.* A unit's long-term performance is usually as good as its training program. Key supervisory support for training can be spotted quickly; ensure that there is an aggressive, well-organized, honest training program with the commander or director heavily involved; it will pay big dividends in performance and morale.

- *Base commander's role.* The final question I ask is, "If this unit could control 100 percent of the base commander's time, in what order of priority would you list things you would have me do to assist in your mission?" The units usually prepared a "dream sheet" of duties and services I could perform to support them. After an orientation visit to each functional area, I selected the most important duties from each list and made a determined effort to organize them into my work schedule. Such a plan made for a busy day, but my people developed a stronger conception that I was working on their behalf.

After completing the orientation briefing, the squadron commander or functional manager would escort me on a walking tour of the entire unit. I sought to shake hands with every member of the air base group. During the visits I was prepared to chat somewhat knowledgeably about their concepts of operation and compliment them on recent major achievements. Since first impressions tend to be lasting, I found the orientation plan helped me get off to a positive start fairly quickly.

Over the years, I have observed many commanders at close range. Both positive and negative examples and considerable study have shaped my own personal philosophy of command.

Train and Delegate

Effective delegation is great therapy for most Air Force organizations. By applying generous doses of time, training, and trust—the three T's—you can move the focus of decision-making down the organization. This practice gets your people involved and frees senior officers for handling the bigger issues. You must let your people know what is expected. You must send a clear, consistent message to your staff indicating what you expect in terms of standards and professional excellence—that you expect them to be experts in their field. Early in the game, I passed along the critical points my boss shared with me. Doing so helped my staff understand the pressures I was experiencing; it helped them understand my decision process.

When I had an experienced and mature staff, I asked for performance in mission-oriented terms; I was not much concerned with methods. This opened an avenue of creativity for them to find better ways of getting the job done. I stressed with equal vigor the responsibility everyone shared in developing subordinates. I frequently asked the colonels—"What have you done recently to help your lieutenants grow?" This subtle pressure served to reinforce professional standards for the senior officers and tended to motivate the junior officers to learn the business more thoroughly.

The open-door policy has become military dictum, but I modified it slightly. My door was open to my staff for informal discussions on problems they were wrestling with in their units. The relationship was that of a coach and player. I rapped with them without giving orders or making the decisions. They could use my experience and background as a nonjudgmental sounding board. If they gave me the problem to solve, I would become a victim of "reverse delegation," which runs counter to our goal of decentralization and subordinate development. This relationship took time to develop, but it provided me a window into the unit and a firsthand view of the subordinate's judgment, values, and decision-making skills.

One other point should be noted with regard to delegating decision-making and action to the lowest level. There are a few situations in which the base commander should be actively involved at the lower-level unit. For example, the headquarters section commander is normally a junior officer with administrative command over enlisted personnel working for senior officers. On occasion, the enlisted personnel have divided loyalties, and, of course, the senior supervisor usually wins out. The base commander needs to do some "down-field blocking" and lend his position power to support his headquarters section commanders.

Positive Reinforcement

The old adage "you spend 90 percent of your time on 10 percent of your people" is true since the chronic troublemakers seem to demand a disproportionate share of a supervisor's time. Consequently, there are only a few minutes a day to recognize and express appreciation to those people accomplishing the mission on a daily basis. Since most of our people are operating at the recognition/self-esteem level, they value sincere positive reinforcement from supervisors.

Not only did I stress public praise when appropriate, I also instituted several positive reinforcement policies. For example, the previous base commander indicated that he was not satisfied with the image and personal appearance of the Security Police Squadron. Part of the problem was that the previous squadron commander had departed PCS several months before and the new commander would not be on board for a few more weeks. A young lieutenant was acting squadron commander. Although he was working the big problems well, the unit was lacking senior leadership. I attended a guard mount shortly after taking command and conducted the usual open-ranks inspection; I could easily understand my predecessor's concern. Fortunately, there was one staff sergeant in the rear rank who looked exceptionally sharp. I stepped in front of him and commented: "Sergeant Dixson, you look exceptionally sharp today. I see your shoes are in good repair and well shined, your trousers are touching the tops of your shoes without a break, your belt is properly adjusted, etc." What I actually did was define a high standard of excellence for everyone in the flight. I concluded with, "You've made an extra effort to be a professional, so I authorize you an extra day off some time within the next 30 days; work out the details with your supervisor." When departing the area in my staff car, I noticed that the flight members were gathering around a beaming sergeant to congratulate him and to learn the new standards. At the next guard mount with another flight, no one's appearance warranted an extra day off. I called the flight chief, a technical sergeant, off to one side. "Sergeant, how do you think your troops look today?" "Oh, they look so-so." "Yes, that's right, and they all look just like you do."

The flight had a three-day break immediately following that shift. It was not until 0600 Sunday morning that I could check them again. When I stepped in front of the flight chief, he saluted proudly. "Sir, B-Flight is prepared for inspection." I could not believe my eyes! Any one of those security policemen could have been used on a recruiting poster. I had a compliment for practically everyone.

I completed my open-ranks inspection and stepped in front of the flight. "Gentlemen, this is, without a doubt, the sharpest, most professional flight of security policemen I have ever inspected. This unit not only has pride but reflects excellent supervision." I addressed the flight chief with, "Sergeant, you have a day off some time within the next 30 days; work out the details with your supervisor." As I departed the area and they were dismissed, there was much backslapping and handshaking. After the arrival of a strong lieutenant colonel commander who also advocated high standards and positive reinforcement, the squadron went on to excel in practically every measure of merit.

Teamwork

I am persuaded that the average person really wants to be part of a successful team—there are very few bona fide "loners." Building team spirit in an air base group staff is challenging because many of the functions do not relate naturally in a mutually supporting way. There may be a tendency for the units to "sub-optimize" performance—enhance their mission at the expense of a sister unit's mission. There are several techniques that can improve the team spirit on such a staff. First, never criticize anyone individually at staff meeting—if you are not pleased with a trend or problem in the group, fuss at the entire staff and press for ways to solve the problem together. Later, when the problem is solved, you can praise the entire group for working the problem successfully. This sets a tone of teamwork.

When one function reported a problem or concern at staff meeting, I would occasionally imply that other units in the group would be happy to help them with the problem—another infusion of "It's not his problem, it's our problem." I also had social functions in my home, allowing functional managers and their spouses to know fellow team members socially.

When tension was noted between two areas, I resolved it; later I would man major projects such as fund drives, committees, etc. with members from those two units. This "forcefeeding" of communications and contact always improved rapport and teamwork.

The bottom line in team building is that the commander is the personal embodiment of the unit's mission. He must be positive and visible to keep his mission positive and visible in the minds of everyone in his unit. The tone and tenor of my actions with my staff were to get them to focus their unit's energy and resources on the broader mission of the entire air base group. There is greater psychological reward when a larger mission is accomplished.

Effective Decision-Making

Very little of a senior commander's daily work involves routine decisions. If so, he has probably centralized decision-making too high in the organization and needs to go back and read about "train and delegate." For the sake of our discussion, let us assume the focus of decision-making is properly established in your unit. What are some guideposts to assist in navigating the rough terrain of executive decision-making?

First, a relationship of absolute candor between a commander and his advisers must exist. The commander can establish an atmosphere that either encourages or discourages open and frank communication. How one handles bad news, disagreements, and mistakes are the keys to turning people into survival-oriented self-servers or mission-oriented team players. I explained to my staff that I had a dubious talent for taking good inputs and making bad decisions, but no one can take poor inputs and make good decisions. I stressed that quality decision-making was a joint venture between the commander and those doing research, developing alternatives, and offering recommendations. The quality, timeliness, and honesty of their work was borne out in the final decision of the boss. I insisted also that they distinguish between facts and opinions; a decision-maker needs both, but he needs them identified accordingly.

The second point to remember in decision-making is to be sensitive to the appropriate decision time. I recalled that during my consulting work a major general asked me to study his staff relationships—he sensed that his staff was rarely genuinely supportive of many of his decisions. He reported that after he had made the final decision, his staff would often ask to "discuss the matter further."

After considerable interviewing with the general and throughout his organization, the following perceptions surfaced: The general felt his role was to make decisions; he abhorred indecisiveness. He remarked proudly, "If anyone comes to me for a decision, he will have one before he leaves my office." The flaw in the staff relationship was poor sensitivity to when a particular decision was actually required. If it were tendered too early, then there were often critical variables that surfaced between when the decision was made and its implementation. In such cases, the staff felt free to "discuss the matter further," and afterwards a different decision was often made. Over time, the staff members were never sure when the general had made a final decision on a subject.

When I discussed this perception with the general at the out-briefing, he agreed completely with the diagnosis and set about to discuss the situation with his staff. He later reported to me that he and his staff benefitted greatly from our suggestions in that area. The first thing you should resolve with your staff in any decision situation is *when* a particular decision should be made. A decision made too early is just as dysfunctional as one made too late.

The next question I ask my staff is, "What are the current limits of my authority in this matter?" I expect them to check the currency of our guidance and advise me of any trends of modifications to current policy. This "window of discretion" is important in evaluating our range of alternatives.

The final question I posed to my staff was (assuming they are oriented to the larger mission of the air base group), "What course of action do you recommend?" It is important for a staff officer to become personally identified with a decision; it tends to improve acceptance and gets him personally involved in the outcome.

The bottom-line understanding I had with my staff was that when they provided me with current, candid inputs with a recommendation focused on the higher mission, then I would take all the "heat" if the decision generated negative repercussions. I found that, on occasion, a senior officer who was not pleased with one of my decisions would register his views with a junior member of my staff. If my decisions were to be discussed with anyone, I was the point of contact. This pledge of downward loyalty generates a reverse effect of upward loyalty to the commander and the mission of his organization.

Summary

It was important to get to know the people and the various aspects of the job. It was critical to clarify what I expect from each subordinate. A practical open-door approach was necessary. High priority was given to the training and development of subordinates, positive reinforcement, effective decision-making, and building teamwork. I'm confident that the combination of these management concepts and approaches made me successful in my new job.

11

ひとつのとつひとつひとつひとつひとつひとつひとつひとつひとつ

Establishing
Variable Work Hours

Changes in personnel policy are frequently made. Usually there is a wide difference in the level of acceptance because people will be affected in different ways. Policies regarding parking, vacations, drinking coffee at desks, smoking, rest periods, lunchtime, and working hours are difficult to develop and implement because of the strong feelings and emotions that people have toward them.

The following case study describes the approach that was taken in a large midwestern insurance company to change working hours. It illustrates a climate where people were seen to be responsible and trustworthy enough to be included in the decision-making process. Communication and participation were used extensively in order to arrive at decisions and get maximum acceptance of a new policy where employees could establish their own working hours.

The philosophy, principles, and approaches that are illustrated in this case would apply to any organization that is considering changes in personnel policy.

Northwestern Mutual Life Insurance Company (NML)
Milwaukee, Wisconsin

*Milford E. Jacobsen, former Vice-President of Personnel and
James W. Ehrenstrom, current Vice-President of Personnel.*

Northwestern Mutual is 119 years old. The home office is in Milwaukee. We are the seventh largest life insurance company with more than 8 billion dollars in assets. We have over 32 billion dollars of life insurance in force. The 1975 sales exceeded 4.6 billion dollars. The business is protecting the financial needs of over 1.2 million policyholders. We specialize in individual life insurance—no group or casualty. We employ 2,000 home office people and are represented by a sales force of over 3,500 full-time agents operating in 49 states. Investment operations are conducted from the home office and 18 mortgage loan and 6 real estate offices located around the country. Our home office non-exempt employees are represented by the Office and Professional Employees International Union which is affiliated with the AFL-CIO.

Our consideration of Variable (we use the term *variable* instead of *flexible*) Hours came about in 1973 because we wanted to institute special summer hours but couldn't get agreement on what they ought to be. Some of us wanted more daylight hours for golf and outdoor activities but not everyone shared our enthusiasm. This started us asking some different questions. "Does it really make any sense to require that everyone come to work and leave at the same time?" "Does it serve either the interests of the firm or its workforce?" Our answer to both questions was "No."

It became apparent that flexibility in work schedules is a key ingredient in satisfying the desire of all of us to influence our own life style. So, we set up a task force made up of one representative from each home office department. Its objective was: "to continue developing a responsive corporate envi-

Note: This description is taken from testimony given to the U.S. Senate Subcommittee on Employment, Poverty, and Migratory Labor on April 7, 1976 in Washington, D.C.

ronment by establishing work schedules that afford maximum selectivity and convenience to our home office employees compatible with operational and service requirements." Note the word, "continue." For years we have been working to create a climate that seems to be present in the most effective organizations: A climate of openness and trust where people are seen as responsible and trustworthy enough to be included in decision making; where employees meet more of their needs, which, in turn, helps the company better meet its goals.

We considered a number of approaches to the rearranged work week but Variable Hours kept bubbling up as the best alternative for us. Employees select the starting time they want, get the approval of the boss, and that becomes their regular work schedule. Our work day is 7½ hours. The only stipulation is that no one can start earlier than 7:00 A.M. or later than 9:00 A.M. With 30 minutes for lunch, that gives us a "core" time of 9:00 A.M. to 3:00 P.M. when all full-time people are at work. Half of our people are at work before 7:30 A.M. and 80 percent of them are in before 8:00 A.M.

Just in case we were getting into something that could backfire, we decided to play it safe by testing the program for 6 months. We were not expecting miracles—we tried to avoid raising the expectations of both the management and non-management groups. We thought our people would like it; it would enhance their image of our company as a great place to work; that it might further improve morale, and possibly improve service to our policyowners and field force. Throughout our 6-month trial period, which ran from October 1, 1973 through April 1, 1974, we measured the effectiveness of our program in terms of service, employee attitudes, supervisory attitudes, the reaction of union officials, tardiness, absenteeism, and morale. We kept all employees informed as to how it was going.

We recognized early in the game that the major accountability for success of the experiment rested with the supervisors. We relied heavily on them to spot and resolve problems—both individually and as a group.

One additional comment about the union. They were in

our corner from the start; we kept them informed during the planning and experimental stages and have never had any resistance from them. It became obvious they thought we had a winner from the start. This was important to us in view of some subsequent changes we made.

We've had variable hours as a way of life for 2½ years. They are great! Almost none of the administrative or operational problems we anticipated have developed. An early task force report stated, "Often what appear to be insurmountable problems can be worked out by employees at their own level if given the opportunity." More job enrichment, if you will.

Some Problems

We have found nothing that has endured as a legitimate limitation to the success of the program. Minor issues pop up and have to be resolved, such as inadequate phone coverage after 3:30 P.M.; apprehension over lack of supervision during certain work hours; some interdepartmental service slowdown; difficulty in scheduling meetings; and employees not understanding that this is a privilege, not a right, and must be compatible with work flow.

A little rearrangement of attitudes is necessary. For example, *someone* will answer the phone after 3:30 P.M. in a work area, but it may not be the familiar voice we are used to hearing. Or, perhaps we can schedule meetings earlier in the day so people won't walk out after 3:00 P.M. We need to be willing to alter some of the inflexible habits that have become comfortable.

Some Advantages

- Most employees think it's marvelous—Jackie no longer sits at her desk reading a paperback from 7:00 to 8:00 A.M. because her husband drops her off on his way to work.
- It's helped make recruitment of new employees easier.
- It's kept NML in the forefront as a progressive employer in the state of Wisconsin.

- Our employees get a lift by talking about it to their friends and acquaintances.
- It's leveled out the 8:00 A.M. and 4:00 P.M. congestion around our building, particularly since a 42-story building has been constructed just across the street.
- It spreads out the traffic flow on city expressways and downtown streets.
- Incoming mail is opened earlier, read, distributed and acted upon earlier in the day.
- It provides an extra hour of telephone service to both east and west coasts.
- It further developed our trust in people to do what is right.
- Supervisors are delegating more management responsibility.
- People see tangible evidence that they are influencing their work situation.
- It is a boost to our affirmative action efforts—a boon to the working mother.
- It stretches our imaginations—has made it more receptive to part-time jobs, job-sharing and other innovative arrangements.
- It's given a good boost to involvement in our company physical fitness program. People can work out their schedules easier and now have fewer valid excuses for avoiding exercise.

Survey Results

Here are some results of a Variable Hours survey we conducted:

A.   Employees were asked:
1.   Should Variable Hours be kept or abandoned?
Eighty-eight percent said keep; only 2 percent said abandon.
2.   Why did you change your hours?
Better fits my personal needs: 43 percent
Avoid traffic and parking problems: 23 percent
Better fits the needs of my family: 21 percent
Car pool did and I had to go along: 5 percent
Other: 8 percent

      3.   What effect has the change had on your performance?
           More Effective: 32 percent
           Less Effective: 1 percent
           No Change: 67 percent

B.   Supervisors were asked:
What has been the effect of Variable Hours on the level of service provided by your division?
Increased the level of service: 36 percent
Decreased the level of service: 6 percent
No effect on the level of service: 58 percent

C.   *Productivity gains.* Our unit cost figures show that we're doing better with Variable Hours than we did without them. In 1975, two critical measures of cost—acquisition of new business and maintenance of business already on the books—were less per $100 of premium than in 1974. Some of the improvement we think is due to Variable Hours.

D.   *Absenteeism, including sick leave.* The first full year of Variable Hours, not counting the experimentation period, was 1975. Our number of days lost per employee, for all reasons, dropped from 5.8 in 1974 to 4.7 in 1975, the lowest average since 1969. That 4.7 days is 1.8 percent for those of you who are used to seeing absenteeism as a percent.

E.   *Employee turnover.* Our non-exempt turnover in 1975 was 13.7 percent—the lowest since World War II. In 1968, our turnover was 33.9 percent, dropped to 17.0 percent by 1974, and then took another dip in 1975. For our type of business, these are rather dramatic figures, on the happy side!

F.   *Tardiness.* We have practically no tardiness anymore! Sounds inviting, doesn't it? It used to be when someone was 10 minutes late, that was just lost time. Now the employee simply makes up the time. Too many instances, of course, and the supervisor just might suggest that they set a new starting time! The company no longer finances tardiness.

G.   *Excused time.* We also stopped subsidizing those extra long lunch hours that involve shopping trips, or dentist appointments, and so on. If Joe has a dental appointment, he can keep it and make up the time that day or during that week. We now get 37½ hours per week on the job out of each full-time employee. They keep themselves honest.

Summary

Variable hours are now part of the everyday climate at NML. They are good for our employees and to paraphrase another businessman's testimony quite a few years ago, "what's good for the employees must be good for the company." And it's such a bargain—it literally doesn't cost anything!

Our experience is totally positive and one of a few changes we've introduced where nobody loses—everybody wins!

Update, March 1984
Lynn F. Bardele, Manager, Personnel Relations

In general, Variable Hours continues to meet the original intent—that is, to provide individual employees with considerable flexibility so they can incorporate their working hours into their daily lives as conveniently as possible, while providing proper staffing and maintaining high service standards. The concept is not "gliding time" wherein there is no set schedule. Instead, employees must select regular hours, with supervisory approval. They continue to have the opportunity to request different hours if their present schedule becomes inconvenient, but we have found that employees generally stay with a schedule once they have selected it. Outside situations such as daycare and car pool arrangements tend to channel people into regular daily patterns.

Further, if employees periodically need flexibility for doctor's appointments, heavy freeway traffic, and so on, daily working schedules can be modified through the use of compensatory time (which allows employees to make up missed time on other days of that week). Of course, if "comp" time is overused to the point that regular working hours are abandoned and the individual's schedule approaches "gliding time," that would be an abuse that would have to be curtailed.

The secondary, and unintended, benefit of Variable Hours is the improved service that the company receives. We have agents and policyowners located throughout the United States and we have heavy telephone contact with them. With Variable Hours, employees start as early as 6:30 A.M. and there are still employees on the job as late as 6:00 P.M. This translates to office hours ranging from 7:30 A.M. on the East Coast, to 4:00 P.M. on the West Coast. Our agents and home office managers find these service hours to be advantageous.

A key factor in the implementation of Variable Hours is trust. When our program was first installed, many managers speculated that they would have to personally be on the job from 7 A.M. until 6 P.M. so that they could monitor all their employees. In some cases our personnel department had to strongly encourage managers to back off and charge their employees with self-responsibility. It works. We don't have time clocks; employees complete time cards on their honor on Monday morning and they feel good about the trust given to them. In fact, employees find the early morning hours and late afternoon hours to be times when they can accomplish sizable volumes of work because there are few incoming telephone interruptions at those times. (Our published "office hours" continue to be 8:10 A.M. to 4:10 P.M.)

The Variable Hours program applies only to nonexempt (nonmanagement) employees. Exempt (management) employees have always had similar flexibility. They operate on the expectation that they will be here as is necessary to get the job done. That gives managers some latitude in scheduling to accommodate personal needs and working-schedule preferences.

Results of a February 1984 survey are shown in Table 2 and Table 3. In addition, it was found that a workweek of 4½

Table 2. Starting Times for Full-Time Regular Employees.
(7½ Hours/Day, Five Days/Week)

Starting Times	Management		Non-management	
Before 6:30 A.M.	2		14	
6:30–6:44	7		12	
6:45–6:59	5		20	
7:00–7:04	31		183	
7:05–7:09	—		2	
7:10–7:14	—		15	
7:15–7:19	11		32	
7:20–7:24	—	258	14	920
7:25–7:29	2	43.2%	19	70.4%
7:30–7:34	67		275	
7:35–7:39	—		4	
7:40–7:44	4		4	
7:45–7:49	25		45	
7:50–7:54	2		8	
7:55–7:59	—		17	
8:00–8:04	99		239	
8:05–8:09	3		17	
8:10	51	51	130	130
		8.5%		9.9%

Table 2. Starting Times for Full-Time Regular Employees, Cont'd.
(7½ Hours/Day, Five Days/Week)

Starting Times	Management		Non-management	
8:11–8:14	7		3	
8:15–8:19	31		26	
8:20–8:24	19		7	
8:25–8:29	24		15	
8:30–8:44	120	261	88	195
8:45–8:59	22	43.7%	9	14.9%
9:00–9:14	34		39	
9:15–9:29	—		1	
9:30–9:44	4		4	
9:45–9:59	—		—	
10:00–after	—		3	
Subtotal	570		1,245	

Table 3. Starting Time Patterns of All Full-Time Regular Employees,
Management and Nonmanagement.

Date of Survey	Before 8:10 A.M.	8:10 A.M.	After 8:10 A.M.	Variable (4½ day week) Schedules
December 1973	48 %	38 %	14 %	None
July 1974	54 %	34 %	9 %	3 %
March 1976	59.6%	21.3%	14.7%	4.4%
September 1977	61.4%	15.7%	17.8%	5.1%
January 1979	63.5%	17.1%	15.9%	3.5%
December 1979	62.8%	17.7%	19.5%	4.5%
December 1980	58.7%	13.8%	19.7%	7.8%
December 1981	59.9%	10.6%	19.3%	10.2%
February 1984	61.9%	9.5%	23.9%	4.7%

days has been selected by 27 (4.5 percent) of the 597 managers
and 62 (4.7 percent) of the 1,307 nonmanagement employees.

The February 1984 survey results can be summarized as
follows:

1. Management employees rather evenly select starting hours
    before and after 8:10 A.M. The favored starting time (21
    percent) is 8:30 A.M.

2. Nonmanagement employees heavily prefer starting before 8:10 A.M. to after 8:10 A.M. (70.4 percent to 14.9 percent). The most prevalent starting time (22 percent) is 7:30 A.M.

3. Since 1976, the numbers of employees starting before 8:10 A.M. have been rather steady, at approximately 60 percent. There also has been a steady increase in the numbers of employees (mostly management) who moved their starting times back from 8:10 A.M. to later times.

4. The 4½-day workweek has been chosen on a regular basis by 4.7 percent of the clerical employees (62 people) and by 4.5 percent of the management employees (27 people).

5. Since all variable hours scheduling for clerical employees continues to be at the discretion of the immediate supervisor, no problems have surfaced with the 4½-day workweek. Management personnel who have chosen the 4½-day workweek have carefully assessed the situation prior to making this selection.

6. Overall, the variable hours concept has continued to be an asset to NML and NML employees. It has allowed the employees to choose work schedules that fit their individual lifestyles and it has increased employee morale as well as service to our agents and policyowners.

12

ⲟⲓⲟ

Improving Productivity Through Work Design

Many organizations are changing the activities, methods, and equipment of employees in order to increase productivity. In many situations, it is strongly resisted by the employees even though change might make the job more interesting, challenging, and rewarding. The following case study illustrates the Motivational Work Design Model developed by Roy W. Walters on how to increase productivity with a maximum of acceptance on the part of employees. This theory maintains that productivity, quality, and job satisfaction can be attained if the job has five core characteristics.

Citibank, New York, New York
Roy W. Walters, Roy W. Walters & Associates,
Mahwah, New Jersey

Motivational Work Design Model

Five core job dimensions provide the key for objectively measuring jobs and changing them so that they have high potential for motivating the people who do them. They can be described as follows:

Toward Meaningful Work. Three of the five core dimensions contribute to a job's meaningfulness for the worker.

- *Skill variety.* The degree to which a job requires the worker to perform activities that challenge skills and abilities. When even a single skill is involved, there is at least a seed of potential meaningfulness. When several skills are involved, the job has the potential of appealing to more of the whole person and of avoiding monotonous repetition of the same task, no matter how much skill it requires.
- *Task identity.* The degree to which the job requires completion of a "whole" and identifiable piece of work, that is, doing a job from beginning to end with a visible outcome.
- *Task significance.* The degree to which the job has a substantial and perceivable impact on the lives of other people, whether in the immediate organization or in the world at large.

Each of these three job dimensions represents one important route to experienced meaningfulness. If the job is high in all three, the worker is quite likely to experience his or her job as very meaningful. It is not necessary, however, for a job to be very high in all three dimensions. If the job is low in any one of them, there will be a drop in overall experienced meaningfulness. Even when two dimensions are low, the worker may find the job meaningful, provided that the third is high enough.

Toward Personal Responsibility. A fourth core dimension may lead a worker to experience increased responsibility in his or her job. This is *autonomy*, the degree to which the job gives a worker freedom, independence, and discretion in scheduling work and determining how it will be carried out. People in highly autonomous jobs know that they are personally responsible for successes and failures. When autonomy is high, how work is performed will depend more on the individual's own efforts and initiatives than on detailed instructions from the boss or from a manual of job procedures.

Toward Knowledge of Results. The fifth core dimension is *feedback.* This is the degree to which a worker is informed of the effectiveness of his or her work activities. Feedback is most powerful when it comes directly from the work itself—for example, when workers have the responsibility for gauging and checking components they have just completed and learn in the process that they have lowered the reject rate by meeting specifications more consistently.

The implementing concepts are specific action steps to improve both the quality of the working experience and the work productivity of the individual. They are as follows:

- *Content analysis.* Examining the content of the job to make sure that irrelevant, redundant operations are not present. This determines whether or not the job is seen as significant by the person performing the work.
- *Task combination.* Combining fragmented tasks into a complete task module. This will provide additional interest, challenge, and a feeling of responsibility for a whole, clearly identified task.
- *Natural work units.* Designing the work according to a logical group that is aligned with the unit's mission. This allows the worker to experience a personal feeling of responsibility and to identify with this group.
- *Client relationship.* Forming relationships with clients representing certain sets of companies within the natural work units. Workers start to call their companies "my customers" and take on a high degree of ownership.
- *Vertical loading.* Pushing responsibilities down from higher levels and giving the workers more control and increased re-

sponsibility. This is done selectively, according to individual competence.

- *Feedback channels.* Setting up conditions for feedback from the work itself is very important in the transition from a one-task job to a partial or a full-task module. Workers and supervisors must know constantly how they are doing in order to improve their work.

Case Study

The following case study illustrates the application of the Motivational Work Design Model in a large bank. It describes how interviews with concerned people allowed management to use empathy in implementing the change. It emphasizes that some changes should be made very slowly to be sure the change is being accepted and implemented.

Two major changes were considered by top management in order to provide customers with a quality product tailored to their needs. These changes were organization around market segments and redesign of clerical jobs.

Organizational Design. Citibank's evolution into a structure focusing on market segments took place over several years. Creating a natural unit of work for an individual job and market segmentation are the same concept applied at different levels of the organization, and either may face constraints that require time phasing. A "natural unit of work" means designing work according to a logical group that is aligned with the unit's mission. In the letter of credit unit, natural work units were structured around market segments, that is, by types of customers—governments, correspondent banks, and branches. These segments were further divided into natural units of work by geographical location, such as Europe, Near East, Far East, and South America.

After "channelization," the structure provided each group head with a natural organization. A channel with all processing functions—from customer input to delivery—vertically integrated under one accountable manager had been developed. Figure 4 shows that separate divisions—marketing, corporate serv-

Figure 4. Citibank's Financial Transaction Services.

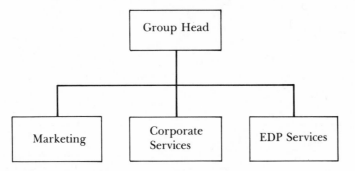

ices, and Electronic Data Processing (EDP) services—were integrated under one group head.

The next major evolution was to more fully develop natural work units by reorganizing into groups facing off against the major market segments: the International Banking Group, the World Corporate Group, and the National Banking Group. Since the marketing department had restructured according to these segments, it was necessary to structure corporate services in the same manner.

The natural work units selected split the marketing department into function processing groups aligned with the major market segments. Each of these groups offered its own services within the group, i.e., loans, collections, letter of credit, money transfer, and so on (see Figure 5).

These groups were, in turn, broken into more clearly identified functions which, at the processing level, are held responsible for servicing certain products. As a result, the organization has created many more fully accountable units, each dedicated to filling the needs of a segmented customer set.

Decentralization of Data Processing. In order to establish these as independent customer organizations, Citibank took advantage of the rapid technological changes in the computer industry. Simply stated, it switched from maxicomputers to minicomputers. Where there had been one centralized data center for the bank, there are now many, each meeting the specific requirements of its own market segments. The bank feels that

Figure 5. Financial Transaction Services of the Marketing Department.

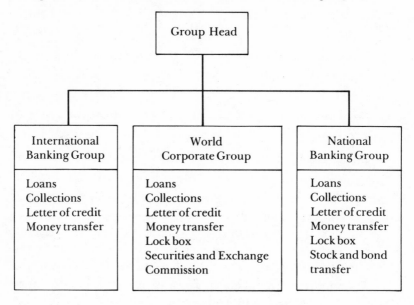

the results over the long term will be dramatic. First, the decentralization will allow considerably more flexibility in the support of specific customer segments. Second, assuming current trends continue, it will be less expensive. Finally, it will enable full accountability by management to the customers it services.

Job Design. It was very clear what the objectives of the first-level job structure should be: service quality to the customer, high level of productivity, minimum personnel problems, and high levels of organization and individual performance. The structure designed was a logical extension of the decentralized organizational structure and envisioned giving each of the clerical staff complete processing and customer-service responsibility for a single, small group of customers. The power of the concept was exciting.

In essence, coupled with the decentralized organizational structure, it would mean that every member of the organization would have customer responsibility for at least one product. The mission of the organization was now the mission of *every* member of the organization. This restructuring held costs constant for a period of time, and the stage was set for the redesign of clerical jobs. The Motivational Work Design was the approach that would be used.

The Motivational Work Design model was taught to all managers and supervisors so they could actively participate and contribute to the work redesign process. The use of this model, together with the organizational changes and the new computer technology, led to the development of a concept called "work station management." This concept gives one clerical employee total responsibility for servicing a single, small group of customers in a defined product area. The employee has a personal computer terminal tied into the division's minicomputer. Emphasis has been placed on a paperless work flow in which the terminal is the key. Filing of documents is on microfilm, and each employee has a film reader in addition to a telephone for immediate client contact. This design benefits employees by providing better jobs and benefits Citibank as well by allowing more control, fewer space requirements, and improved customer service.

Letter of Credit Unit. The letter of credit unit was organized on a functional basis, with the processes of payment examination, processing, filing, issuing/amending, customer service, and accounting each representing distinct organizational entities within the channel, as shown in Figure 6.

The next step was the realignment of the channel around the types of customers dealt with: governments, correspondent banks, and branches. Within this organization, however, the assembly-line work flow was maintained, as shown in Figure 7.

The next step entailed a detailed process review, or content analysis, to ensure that both managers and supervisors had complete understanding and control over the manual, labor-intensive work flows prior to automation.

After this thorough analysis, the management team decided that the only way to fully understand the process was under controlled conditions in a laboratorylike environment. The team created the "white room," a separate walled-off area in the letter of credit unit, and put in it all the equipment

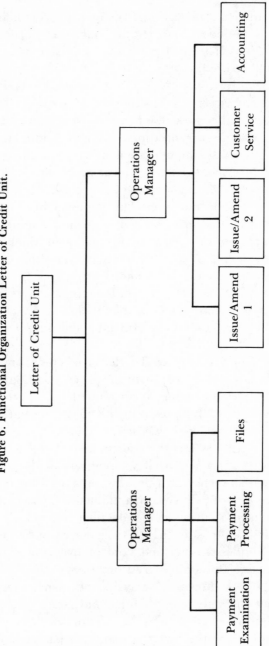

Figure 6. Functional Organization Letter of Credit Unit.

Figure 7. Organizational Chart.

Government	Correspondent Banks	Branches
Files	Files	Files
Mail Services	Mail Services	Mail Services
Payables Processing	Payables Processing	Payables Processing
Payment Processing	Payment Processing	Payment Processing
Accounting	Accounting	Accounting

Customer Service

needed to process a letter of credit: typewriter, adding machine, forms, rubber stamps. As pieces of the assembly-line process were put together, they were thoroughly tested in the "white room." This "room" was a computer facility for testing pieces of the manual-processing function to determine whether or not they could be computerized. Software programs were written for processing functions, such as *preprocessing, encoding, amending,* and *issuing,* and trials were run to determine whether they could be eliminated as separate manual functions.

It made a splendid testing ground for measuring the difference between what was written as an existing practice and procedure and what was being done in actual processing. It was an area in which to experiment on what might be. In a short time, the managers were able to reduce the steps required in processing by half and to reduce the number of people in the processing operation by 30 percent—all before automation.

Richard Matteis and Sandra Jaffee, the two vice-presidents who guided the redesign effort, state that the "white room" concept was an important step in the conversion to a more effective work system. They are convinced that this step should always be taken to permit thorough experimentation prior to any system changes, to maintain management control, and to allow for critical examination of details that might otherwise have been overlooked.

Automation was implemented piece by piece, only after the affected processes had been streamlined. Once the processes were completely automated, the training effort required to combine the assembly-line functions into the work station job was begun. This combination yielded the letter of credit work station shown in Figure 8.

Figure 8. Letter of Credit Work Station.

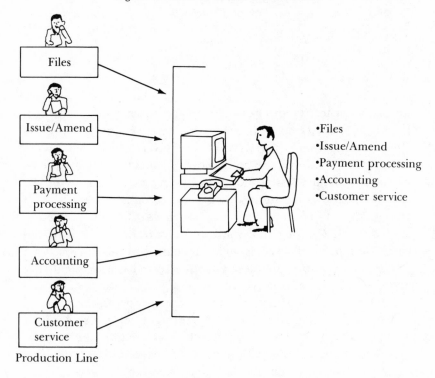

Production Line

The Work Stations. To support this job redesign, a physical environment was developed in which all the tools necessary to perform the job were at the fingertips of the work station representative: a cockpit type of furniture design, which contained a data entry cathode ray terminal (CRT), a microfilm reader, and a telephone. The work stations were in a pleasant, open space and grouped in clusters by customer aggregate. The "back office," in essence, had all of the amenities of the front office and was professional in nature.

In the original diagnostic work that was necessary to determine the details of the operation problems and the type of organization climate that would support the change effort, about one hundred interviews with key managers, supervisors, and workers were conducted. It was necessary to get firsthand information about the employees' attitudes toward their work as well as toward change.

It was obvious that none of those interviewed liked the way the current processing flow was operating. They all felt the pressure from backlogs, unmet schedule dates, error rework, customer complaints, and so on. Managers and supervisors thought the workers were not performing well, and the workers felt they were not being utilized well. Workers also felt that system procedures were an impediment to improving the operation and did not permit them to make contributions to their work. The morale of both groups was very low.

When managers and supervisors were asked to conceptualize the type of employee qualified to operate a newly designed single job that would contain *all* the functional processing pieces, none of them believed that the current workers would be able to perform this theoretical job. They said that the job would require workers of a much higher caliber, probably from the country's top graduate business schools. However, they were willing to experiment with other models.

Their reaction was not uncommon. Managers and supervisors often fail to understand that the performance of subordinates is predicated on what they have been given to do. If their work is simple, repetitive, and narrow in scope, their performance will be just that. Thus, any effort to conceptualize employees as adequate for a more complicated, expanded job will usually result in negative reactions. Simply put, people will do better jobs when they have better jobs to do.

It was suggested that the employees train one another so that each would become familiar with all the functions required by the new job. This proved to be successful and eliminated the need for a large central staff of skilled trainers. Employees took a great deal of pride in teaching others the details of their function and in learning the details of all the other functions. They were enthusiastic about the process as this cross-training effort got under way. In the few instances where workers could not master all the functions required in the new job, they were moved to other locations in the bank.

Managers and supervisors were all educated in work-effectiveness concepts and collectively designed the new work station. Employees who could acquire the knowledge and skills to operate the new work station were also involved in the testing process used in the "white room", and, ultimately, in the new design.

The letter of credit unit was the starting point. Since the institutionalization of this new configuration, other divisions (for example, money transfer and lock box) have gone the same route. These changes have been made slowly and with deliberate care. Five years is not a long time for such sizable change.

The impact of this new environment on employees has been significant. Instead of being cogs in a wheel, each is a manager of services. The jobs have variety, interest, and importance, and the people who perform them can see the results of their efforts.

The measurement of the motivating potential of this job has clearly demonstrated that the desired job characteristics of skill variety, task identity, autonomy, task significance, and feedback are present to a greater extent in this job than in a functional position. For example, the International Banking Group (IBG) letter of credit work station had a motivating potential score of 134.9 versus a 47.96 in the IBG treasury preparer position, as measured by a job diagnostic survey devised by the author. Therefore, if the theory base is valid, the desired results of productivity, service quality, and job satisfaction should accrue at Citibank.

Revenues nearly quadrupled while expense remained constant over a five-year period. During this time, staff size was reduced by 80 percent.

The letter of credit unit of the International Banking Group was the starting point. It took one and a half years to move from the manual system to the work-station format. Since that initial effort, the concepts have spread across other operational units. This has required additional time, but the results in other units have been equally dramatic.

Both Matteis and Jaffee emphasize that such radical changes cannot and should not be made quickly. They have learned about the complexities inherent in organizational development issues and refrain from forcing the issue. Even with the total of close to seven years required, Jaffee feels that they may have moved too quickly.

The work effectiveness concept is a tool any organization can use to develop improvements in cost, income, or staff size. It is a tool that is controlled by management rather than by those outside of management. It can be adopted at the top level of an organization or in a lower-level department. That is a decision of management.

The objective of work effectiveness is to provide managers with tools they can use to improve organizational productivity and effectiveness. At Citibank, managers have used these tools to do exactly that—with results that are self-evident.

Reflections on Change at Citibank.

- *Why.* The bank faced a deteriorating service problem and the operations costs had risen sufficiently high to make profit meager or nonexistent. Pricing differentials for the variety of services offered is of little consequence in the banking business. They all price about the same, so business goes to that organization that can produce timely, accurate service.
- *What.* Any change required significant revision of the design of jobs and the way the work flowed through the operation. Adding more people and machinery *would not* solve the problem. A strategy was required that would lead toward this revision and not be viewed as something that management was "laying on" the people. Involving the managers/supervisors/workers in the change effort offered the best opportunity for gaining support of the people through vested ownership of the change process.
- *How.* The change required three main activities—diagnosis, education, and implementation.
    1. *Diagnosis.* This included extensive interviews at all levels, flow charting of work processes, observations, exam-

ination and analysis of organization charts, policies, and procedures.

2. *Education.* This consisted of three days of intensive communication and education on theoretical models of work design (work effectiveness model), practice cases, and finally focus on their own jobs.

3. *Implementation.* The knowledge gained in the education phase was put to use. Problems were analyzed and solutions developed for change. All this was done with regard to any specific action step's impact on other work functions or processes. Participation was used throughout the implementation.

- *Time.* The entire change of the total operations section required a time span of six years. The work force was reduced from 10,000 to 4,500. No person was fired. Hiring was frozen, and attrition, combined with some movement to other bank functions, reduced the force.

13

⟲⟳⟲⟳⟲⟳⟲⟳⟲⟳⟲⟳⟲⟳⟲⟳⟲⟳⟲⟳⟲⟳⟲⟳⟲⟳⟲⟳⟲⟳⟲⟳⟲⟳⟲⟳⟲⟳

Successfully Implementing Quality Circles

Quality circles is a formal way of getting participation from employees in order to solve departmental problems. It originated in Japan and has been implemented without modification in many U.S. organizations. Many other organizations have modified the concept to fit their situation. The objectives of quality circles are to arrive at decisions regarding change and to get a maximum degree of acceptance. The many success stories prove that both objectives can be accomplished. The final decision regarding the change is made by higher management. The quality circles only recommend. However, because they have thoroughly analyzed problems, considered many possible solutions, and reached agreement on the best solution, nearly all of their recommendations are accepted by higher management and implemented. The commitment to the decision by the members of the circle is almost automatic.

One of the pioneers and leaders in the field is Sud Ingle, who introduced a quality circle program into Mercury Marine in 1978. Since then, he has introduced it into other organizations, written books, developed slides, and taught seminars on the subject. For this book, he has outlined some principles and described two specific cases where he has installed programs. Each case illustrates a high degree of participation in deciding on changes and implementing them successfully.

Mercury Marine Division, The Brunswick Corporation,
Fond du Lac, Wisconsin, and Saint Agnes Hospital,
Fond du Lac, Wisconsin
Sud Ingle, Quality Circle Consultant
Fond du Lac, Wisconsin
(former Director of Quality Control, Mercury Marine)

In the 1970s, many American companies were facing critical problems of low productivity and high cost due to high ris-
ing prices of oil, soaring inflation, and poor management practice. At the same time, Japan had begun to conquer the world's
markets for automobiles, computers, television, and other products. In 1974, upon carefully observing Japanese management
systems, Americans started to install quality circles (Q.C.) in
their organizations. During the next five years, the growth of
this concept exploded. By 1983, there were 6,000 organizations
using Q.C. concepts to create teamwork and build employee involvement in improving quality of the organization.

The success of quality circles in manufacturing industries
attracted the service organizations. They quickly found that this
people-building philosophy had great application for:

1. Hospitals and health care organizations.
2. Banks and financial institutions.
3. Transportation and hospitality.
4. Public utilities.
5. Government agencies.
6. Associations.
7. Wholesale and retail stores.
8. Governmental units.

Definition

Quality circles can be defined as a small group of people
doing similar work, meeting regularly to identify, analyze, and
solve problems in their work area. Q.C. programs have several
major characteristics:

1. Circles meet regularly at the scheduled time.
2. Participation is voluntary.
3. Average size of a group is six to eight.
4. Problems are identified, analyzed, and solved by the circle.
5. Suggested solutions are then presented to higher management for approval and action.

A sound, carefully thought-out implementation plan is necessary for effective introduction of a quality circle program in an organization. It should include the following:

1. Study the concept to see if it will work in the organization.
2. Visit quality circle programs in other organizations.
3. Make a decision to start.
4. Select and train a facilitator/coordinator.
5. Form a steering committee of upper-level management.
6. Develop plans and goals.
7. Communicate the plan to management and the union if there is one.
8. Form circles (get volunteers).
9. Train circle leaders and members.
10. Check progress monthly.

Mercury Marine and Brunswick Corporation

The quality circles program started at Mercury Marine in 1978 with the following objectives:

1. Improve quality.
2. Reduce waste.
3. Improve communication.
4. Teach group problem-solving techniques.
5. Increase worker satisfaction.

The quality circles program began on a pilot basis in two of its plants in Wisconsin and Florida, with five circles at each location. In January 1979, the program was expanded to include 1,200 trained circle members and more than one hundred circles. Each year, new circles were formed at the various Mercury Marine plants. Following Mercury Marine's lead, other divisions of Brunswick Corporation implemented quality circle programs. Participation in the circles is voluntary. Discussion is geared strictly toward solving production problems in a given work area. Some of the problems solved by the circles are as follows:

- Florida circles eliminated a costly deburring process. This group confronted a problem of burrs that developed on certain aluminum pieces when drilled. Discussion by group members led to the suggestion that a softer aluminum alloy might eliminate burrs, thereby eliminating the costly necessity for deburring afterwards. This idea proved to be correct and the recommendation was accepted by higher management and implemented.
- The Trolling MERC circles simplified assembly training operation by organizing and coordinating about one hundred photographs of the process showing step-by-step assembly procedures to be followed. They also achieved zero defects in Thruster assembly inspection during regular production.
- At the main MERC assembly plant in Fond du Lac, quality circle members analyzed the problem of piston damagers at one production point. The circle recommended that bumpers be installed to prevent the pistons from falling out of a processing oven. Implementation of that idea and a related suggestion to prevent the bearing from becoming lodged in piston assemblies has eliminated damage to pistons.
- At the Lancer Division's facility in Bridgeton, Missouri, a circle made a process more efficient by changing the equipment in the bottling line.
- The employees at the Brunswick Division in Eminence, Kentucky, made more efficient use of available floor space by correcting loose stitching on one type of bowling bag.
- At the Defense Division facility in Marion, Virginia, employees launched a defect reduction program, a variation of

quality circles. The aim of this program was to involve employees who work on radomes for the General Dynamics F-16 aircraft in efforts to reduce defects. It was successful from both a production and employee morale standpoint.

Saint Agnes Hospital

Saint Agnes Hospital in Fond du Lac, Wisconsin, formed Employee Participation Circles (EPC) in the fall of 1980. Top management believed that the employees know the most about the problems in their work areas and that a circle program will provide them a channel for recommending solutions.

Some of the objectives of their program were:

1. Improvement in patient care services.
2. Improvement in hospital-wide communications.
3. Improvement in morale and job satisfaction.
4. Improvement in cost containment and/or efficiency efforts.

After EPC members underwent the training, they formed four circles to pursue these objectives. To get the program off the ground, two nursing units and two laboratories were chosen to participate in the pilot program. A cross section of participants such as RNs, LPNs, technicians, nursing assistants, and unit clerks were involved in the voluntary membership of the circles.

To ensure success, the circles focused on specific steps:

1. Identify the problem.
2. Gather data on the specific part.
3. Analyze the gathered data and sort out the factual data.
4. Determine the corrective measures to solve the problems.
5. Develop a plan for implementing the corrective measures.
6. Present the recommendations to higher management for approval and action.

Using these criteria, these circles worked on different projects and came up with changes such as:

1. A time-efficient method of assembling admission packs.
2. A new manual for consistent training for all new phlebot-
   omists.
3. A list of duties for nursing assistants so that the nurses'
   time would be used more efficiently.
4. An updated list of medication and narcotics that are being
   used by doctors for their patients and a new procedure to
   keep the list up-to-date.

Possible Problems with Quality Circles

Problems in any new program are not unusual. And problems can cause serious setbacks if not properly resolved. The
problems that organizations may face in managing Q.C. programs include the following:

1. Insufficient support from top management.
2. Lack of cooperation from middle management.
3. Discouragement because of unrealistic expectations.
4. Lack of support and even opposition from the union.
5. Poor selection of the facilitator and circle leaders.
6. Poor circle performance because of insufficient training.
7. Interference from noncircle members to deter the circle
   operation.
8. Unwillingness of members to participate in the discussions.
9. Desire for personal credit for individuals rather than a desire for circle achievement.
10. Overly talkative members making Q.C. meetings nonpro-
    ductive.
11. Lack of enthusiasm because of inadequate publicity.
12. Poor communications.

Keys to a Successful Program

In order to have a successful Q.C. program, the following
key points must be kept in mind:

1. *Proper atmosphere.* To create a healthy atmosphere, an organization should be sure that:
   - The philosophy of participative management is accepted by people at all levels of the organization including management, union leaders, and nonmanagement employees.
   - Basic philosophy of the program is known to everyone in the organization before starting the program.
   - Positive aspects of the process are stressed and achievements publicized properly.
2. *Support from top management.* In addition to believing that participative management is good, members of top management must give the program active support by:
   - Communicating their approval.
   - Participating actively on the steering committee.
   - Listening to and acting on the recommendations of the circles.
   - Giving recognition to those who contribute.
3. *Enthusiastic facilitator.* A quality circle facilitator's job is not easy. There are ups and downs in the process. The facilitator must:
   - Maintain enthusiasm for the program.
   - Be helpful to Q.C. leaders and members at all times.
   - Listen closely to all persons involved including management and circle members.
   - Demonstrate a caring nature.
   - Give credit where due.
4. *Systematic training.* The circle members as well as management personnel need to undergo formal Q.C. training to learn how to identify, analyze, and solve the problems systematically.
5. *Slow, systematic growth.* For a new concept such as Q.C., it is wise to proceed slowly, as follows:
   - Choose a few projects to start with.
   - Form a few pilot circles.
   - Choose the right area for the formation of circles.
   - Always keep the participation voluntary.
   - Be open and positive about circle's activities.

6. *Good follow-up and evaluation system.* With the proper supervision from the facilitator and with elements of trust and mutual cooperation, the Q.C. program should run smoothly. But it is still important that the facilitator, with the help of the steering committee, tabulate the progress of the program systematically. This includes projects completed, money saved, saving of human effort and time, and reduction in waste. This should be done on a regular basis.

7. *Recognition.* It is very important to remember that this is a people-building philosophy. And people as a team make the program work. The achievements accomplished are of the circles and not of its leader, facilitator, or a particular member. Circles must be credited for their accomplishments through proper publicity and other forms of recognition and rewards.

Quality circles have proven to be a successful way to get participation from employees. Where it has been properly planned and implemented, the results include:

1. Improvement in quality.
2. Improvement in productivity.
3. Improvement in interdepartmental communication.
4. Less absenteeism.
5. Fewer accidents.
6. More job satisfaction.
7. Reduction in costs.
8. Reduction in scrap and waste.
9. Improved team spirit and teamwork.
10. A substantial return on investment (average ratio of six to one).
11. More job security.

14

ଠାଠାଠାଠାଠାଠାଠାଠାଠାଠାଠାଠାଠାଠାଠାଠାଠାଠାଠାଠ

Getting More Productivity from the Last Hour of Work

One of the most difficult changes to implement is one that replaces a past practice with a new policy that will require people to put forth more effort. Such was the situation in the case described in this chapter. In this case, upper-level management recognized a problem and decided it had to be corrected. They recognized that both supervisors and employees would probably be opposed to it. They tried to communicate to the supervisors and sell them on the need to change, but the supervisors resisted. Finally, through extensive participation, the situation was corrected with a high degree of acceptance on the part of both supervisors and workers.

Paterno Company, Houston, Texas
Robert Blake and Jane Mouton,
Scientific Methods, Inc., Austin, Texas

Employees in one plant of this organization had fallen into the habit of slacking off during the last hour of work. Supervisors were aware of this and were under a good deal of pressure from their managers to do something about it. Privately they acknowledged it as a real problem, but in fact they did nothing. Rather, they scheduled themselves into their offices during the last hour of the day under the guise of using that hour for planning the next day's work. The result was that they didn't have to see the problem. At first, the supervisors felt it was a temporary situation and would correct itself. However, it continued for three years and became a chronic problem.

An unusual situation existed that complicated the problem. Employees had work-related justifications for being away from their primary area and in contact with employees in different sections. Thus, employees in any supervisory area might be supervised by that area's supervisor or by a supervisor from another area.

Diagnosing the Situation

In diagnosing the situation, management realized that the problem was out of control. Original policy had been replaced by a norm that legitimized slacking off as a way of slowing down. The problem reflected poor management. It also had an adverse effect on morale and productivity because employees lined up in front of the time clock instead of staying at their work place until it was time to punch out.

Rather than exercise responsibility for achieving productivity, none of the supervisors took corrective action to rectify the problem in their department. Each one intuitively sensed that to take such an action would be unpopular and would probably bring criticism from both supervisory colleagues and from employees for trying to win points with management.

The diagnosis went beyond these considerations because

supervisors were hiding in their offices during the last hour of work in order to have an excuse for not doing something about the problem. They understood that if their boss never saw them in the area where social activities were taking place, no manager could complain that the supervisor "was right there and saw the problem and did nothing about it." This was particularly true if supervisors could justify their absence from the field of activity because they were "planning tomorrow's work."

The problem of slacking off was seen to represent a breakdown in supervisory effectiveness. Needed was the establishment of a new norm, accepted fully by all supervisors, so that each could feel support from the others in acting more responsible in solving the problem. With such a norm in place, any supervisor who failed to exercise responsibility for correcting the problem would become the deviant. The problem, therefore, was to help supervisors replace the "do nothing" norm with a norm of shared responsibility for maintaining productivity throughout the workday.

Twenty supervisors reported to four managers. Over the last several years, the managers repeatedly discussed the problem among themselves. Different approaches to its resolution were attempted one after another, all without measurable success. One approach called for each manager to talk to his or her supervisors and explain the importance of having people apply their efforts during the last work hour. Each manager did this and requested each supervisor's help in resolving the difficulty. Nothing happened.

A second approach discussed by the managers was whether a symbolic firing of one or two supervisors might not signal to the rest that "we mean business." If this "message" could get through to the supervisors, it might settle the problem once and for all. This solution was not applied, however, because of fear that such firings would be demoralizing and would lead to even further reduction in productivity. Another possible approach was to employ two new supervisors who were not party to the past practices and who would therefore be freer to take the lead in bringing about needed changes.

Other possible solutions were discussed or tried, but none

provided a satisfactory resolution of the problem. Finally, management made a determined effort to turn things around and instituted a series of meetings. The participants in this case were the twenty supervisors. They were in a position to resolve the problem and it was their responsibility to do so. Moreover, all of them needed to be involved in formulating and maintaining the new norm.

Identifying the Problem

The first action of the supervisors was to identify the causes of the problem in response to the following questions written on flip-chart paper: "What is the cause of the slacking-off problem? How can it be corrected?" Supervisors convened during the last hour of work to deal with these questions. Since the "do nothing" norm was shared by all the supervisors, they were gathered together in two leaderless groups of ten to discuss the problem.

It wasn't difficult for the discussion to get going. One supervisor said, "Attitudes toward work have changed. It's not like the old days. People expect to find more enjoyment nowadays and that's why they slow down." Another said, "The workers are older now. They feel their jobs are secure. They don't have to prove that they are hard workers. They know that they have jobs that will carry them to retirement if they wish to stay aboard." A third said, "The work they do isn't terribly interesting. Concentrating on it seven hours is a pretty good achievement. Slowing down during the last hour is very understandable." A fourth said, "The real problem is the new generation. It has a more casual attitude than the last generation and it has infected everyone. It's a hopeless situation."

The "them-ism" problem was apparent. Each supervisor was putting the blame on "them." Each of the "them-ism" explanations was recorded on a flip chart for all to see. Finally, a different explanation was offered tentatively by one of the supervisors, who said, "When you come right down to it, the problem is that we're not supervising." Another quickly said, "Don't write that down. We don't want anybody to see that!"

As the discussion continued, participants returned to the "we're not supervising" explanation of the problem. Someone else then asked, "If we are not supervising, why aren't we supervising? We are paid as supervisors." The discussion had now identified the "do nothing" norm. Each participant could verify it in terms of his or her own experiential reality.

The discussion became more involved as the supervisors zeroed in on their own feelings. Someone said, "I know that none of you will do anything about the problem, and therefore if I do, all I'll get in return is kidding by the rest of you and criticism by employees. Why should I expose myself to that kind of hassle when I don't have to?" Others readily agreed. The general feeling emerged that none of the supervisors was confident of the readiness of other supervisors to come to grips with the problem. The cause had finally been identified.

Action Planning for Resolution

The next meeting dealt with exploring solutions to the problem. After some discussion, one supervisor made the following point: "I'm willing to take the initiative in solving the problem in my area, but only if the rest of you are willing to do likewise in your areas. I'm not going to do it if you're not going to." This comment introduced a very intense discussion of the extent to which supervisors would be willing to commit themselves to a new norm related to maintaining productivity throughout the workday. Some supervisors were reluctant to commit themselves to it for fear of a backlash.

As the meeting continued, the new norm began to emerge, but it was obvious that supervisors were unprepared to give their support to it until they had explored how it might be implemented. As the possibility of bringing this new norm into use was discussed, the notion was developed that implementation should take place in a stepwise way. Much discussion led to the formulation of the following action plan.

- *Week 1.* Every supervisor meets with his or her employees to announce that supervisors across the organization have agreed that it is their responsibility to provide leadership in solving the slacking-off problem. Supervisors have uniformly committed themselves to doing so. During this week supervisors ask employees to talk with one another and hopefully to give favorable consideration to helping supervisors bring the problem to a constructive solution.

- *Week 2.* Supervisors begin implementing the new norm by becoming active in their work areas. When they see someone being sociable in an unproductive way, they ask the person to return to work but take no further action.
- *Week 3.* Supervisors ask each person they see socializing in an unproductive way to get back to work, and they record the person's name if they know it, or ask the person his or her name if they don't know it. They report the person's name to the appropriate supervisor.
- *Week 4.* If the problem persists, the supervisors interview those who are socializing in an unproductive way in order to make sure that the slackers understand the seriousness of the intent to solve the problem.
- *Week 5.* If an employee persists in slacking off, a letter is placed in the file as a documentation preparatory to disciplinary action.
- *Week 6.* If the behavior continues, the supervisor takes disciplinary action.

Development of this action plan proved to supervisors that a positive solution was feasible. By this time all supervisors had committed themselves to the new norm and to its implementation.

Implementing the Plan

During the first two weeks, the slacking-off phenomenon became the butt of considerable joking, not only among the hourly personnel but also between the workers and their supervisors. Remarks were made like "Am I being sociable or is this a legitimate problem for us to be discussing?" However, it was evident that the announcement by the supervisors that they were committed to solving the problem was enough to clear the air and develop a widely shared positive attitude toward improving the situation. A few nudgings were necessary during the third week, but the problem had diminished to such a degree that no interviews were necessary, no letters of documentation were placed in the files, and no disciplinary action was needed.

The supervisors reconvened twice to review the situation— once at the end of the third week and once at the end of the seventh week. They experienced great satisfaction that the problem had been solved and, beyond that, saw the importance of leading employees in a responsible way and supporting one another in the process of doing so.

The opposite of a backlash effect was observed because morale seemed to improve among supervisors and employees alike. One employee said, "To tell the truth, I always felt a little guilty toward the end of the day. I knew it wasn't quite right, but everyone else was doing it so I joined the gang. In fact, the time goes more rapidly when we stay busy."

This approach to the slacking-off problem is a good example of how norm shifting can be used to replace a "do nothing" norm that had been held in place by distrust. Any effort to solve the problem without replacing the "do nothing" norm was bound to have been unsuccessful simply because the true cause of the problem had not been diagnosed. Bringing the distrust that supervisors felt toward one another into focus provided the necessary insight and motivation to deal constructively with the real issue.

15

ΟΙΟΙΟΙΟΙΟΙΟΙΟΙΟΙΟΙΟΙΟΙΟΙΟΙΟΙΟΙΟΙΟΙΟΙΟΙΟΙΟΙΟΙΟ

Gaining Acceptance
for a New Incentive System

Any change that has an effect on job security and pay is very difficult to implement without causing a lot of resistance. The following case study illustrates the careful planning and implementation of a new incentive/piecework system. It describes an organization that had a great concern for its employees and considered them its most important asset. The empathy for its employees was constantly present as the change was made. The case also illustrates the effective use of both communication and participation in deciding on the specific change and getting it implemented with a high degree of acceptance. The organization decided that its name should not be made public.

A Massachusetts Manufacturer of Electronic Systems
Richard W. McCarthy, Management Consultant,
Ashby, Massachusetts

The company has been manufacturing low-technology electrical-mechanical devices since 1890. In the 1960s and 1970s high-technology electronic systems were added to the product line. The company was a leader in its field but found that it was gradually losing market share, quality was slowly deteriorating, profits were still very good but the trend lines were not, and manufacturing systems had been virtually untouched since World War II. This was particularly true of an incentive/piecework system that had been installed in the 1940s and received no maintenance for the next thirty-five years.

To keep the system going and to see that the employees were paid a fair rate, first-line supervisors found that they had to manipulate the system by inserting incorrect data. Since the incentive/piecework system was considered a sacred cow, the supervisors were encouraged to "keep the system working" and no questions were asked about how they did it.

There was no industrial engineering department. Two time study people used a watch to set rates that ranged from too tight for the best worker to make the rate to so loose that it cost the company a sizable amount of money. Further, production was run on the false assumption that if incentive workers were idle, they did not cost any money.

The first step was to conduct an audit to determine the possible cost savings that could result from productivity improvement. Because there were no qualified people in the company to conduct the audit, a consulting firm that specialized in industrial engineering and incentive/piecework systems was engaged. In a few weeks the consultants were able to establish that the company had the opportunity to achieve productivity improvements from $300,000 to $1,000,000 annually. This data agreed with the estimates that the vice-president of manufacturing had already developed. The potential savings were so large that management quickly gave approval to proceed with the proposed plan.

Both the vice-president of manufacturing and the director of personnel were convinced that such savings were not achievable until they could establish the following facts in the minds of all: that the revised systems would be fair, that all employees would have equal opportunities to earn a decent wage, that the rates would be tough but achievable and the same for all, that skilled work would be recompensed appropriately, that equal job opportunities would be open to all, that a fair and consistent pay system would be put in place, and that seniority would be given considerable weight. They felt that the company could win the approval and support of employees and managers only by being totally fair, honest, consistent, and above all, open with everyone.

The first step was to form a steering committee, cochaired by the vice-president of manufacturing and the director of personnel. They controlled the assets in the form of time, dollars, and manpower that were vital to the success of the project. Further, both cochairs reported to the chief operating officer, ensuring the access to the highest level of management that was necessary for success. Other members of the steering committee were the production superintendent, the manager of production engineering, and the manager of manufacturing cost accounting. The consultant, also a member, was expected to make sure the agenda was set and to be a stimulator and mediator when tough subjects were being avoided or discussed. Initially, the steering committee held daytime meetings (some running into the evening hours) off premises to guarantee no interruptions.

The composition and size of the steering committee was one of the keys to its success. The most crucial action by the committee was the establishment of small task forces and pilot groups, generally with a very short life span. This was done effectively because the cochairs could assign their people and control the setting of priorities. It was through the task forces and pilot groups that the committee was able to maximize the number of people involved in the change process and later in the implementation of the decisions. Without that involvement at all levels, the degree of success desired would never have been achieved.

Early in the process, the cochairs decided to hold meetings with all hourly personnel. A schedule of over forty meetings, averaging twenty-two people per meeting, was established in order to reach all 900 employees. Through these meetings, all concerned employees became involved in the process. Further, many of them made major contributions to the success of the multiple projects by identifying the deep concerns of the employees, by unearthing problems that management was not even aware of, by indicating pitfalls that had to be overcome, and by acting as a constant barometer for the entire life of the projects. These meetings enabled the committee to pinpoint those factors that would help ensure the success of the projects and, even more important, those factors that had to be addressed and resolved if there was to be any chance of success.

It is important to note that both cochairs continued to stay in regular communication with the employees by "walking around the factory" for an hour or two daily. By showing their willingness to come to the employee to listen intently and to answer their questions, creditability was being firmly established. This was true even though many of the answers were not what the employees wanted to hear. The vital fact was that they got their questions answered and they got them answered quickly.

Through honest, open communication, employees' opinions were genuinely solicited and they were treated with dignity and respect. By doing this, management was building an image that said it cared, common goals were being developed, and values were being established that were meaningful and would be a common ground when everyone came together. This was achieved by living it on a daily basis, not by a one-shot special program.

Similar meetings were held with the foremen who felt most threatened by the change. The cochairs were able to get the foremen to develop their own litany of horrors about the incentive system. It was fairly easy for them to agree intellectually that the system should be changed; it was very difficult for them to accept the change emotionally. A whole way of life was being threatened and many could not deal with the discomfort and problems that might result.

It was very important to address the emotions of the employees and to see and understand their perception of management. The steering committee realized that many managers would be upset when they found that their people's perceptions of them were not in keeping with their own image. The acceptance of this truth was necessary to stimulate further upward communication and to achieve the level of success needed. Effective change can only occur when management has a genuine empathy for all employees, where two-way communication is established and maintained, where people feel actively involved in the change process, and where dignity and respect for the individual are the norm. It was this kind of a value structure that the vice-president of manufacturing and the director of personnel were building. It became the foundation from which all else flowed.

The president was very proud of the long history of success of the company and was genuinely concerned about the old-timers in particular. There were many long-service people who regarded their seniority as their most important possession. Thus, the cochairs regarded it as vital to present crucial issues far in advance, to have the hard decisions agreed to, to deliberately remind top management of that which they had approved, and to promise the president that there would not be any surprises at the last minute.

The following examples illustrate the specifics of what was done. The revised incentive system was designed to produce a bell curve where 100 percent productivity was the minimum acceptable, 125 percent was the norm, and a few high achievers might hit 170 to 180 percent. The key issue was the ability of each employee to make at least 100 percent. If they were below 100 percent, a review was made of the rate, setup, methods, and materials. If all of these were correct and the employee could not be helped via training to reach 100 percent, the employee had to be transferred to a job where 100 percent could be achieved. Since this usually meant a reduction in pay and because some high-seniority people had been identified earlier as probably being on jobs for which they were not qualified, this had the potential of being a major issue. In reviewing this issue with management, it was agreed to protect the employment, but not necessarily the specific job, of all employees. It was fair to both the company and the individual to find them a job where they could be successful, rather than leaving them exposed to embarrassment and failure on a job they could not handle.

A second major issue was how to treat people who had a "red circle rate" (paid above the maximum rate for that job) when the company granted general increases. Should their rate be frozen until the rate line caught up with them? (If this was done, some might never receive another raise.) Should they receive a partial increase? Should they receive the full increase? It is important to note that if "red circle" persons receive no increase, then the rate would continue to be a red circle rate from six to eight years. If they received a partial increase, the life span of the red circle would increase to a range of seven to twelve years.

It was decided that because seniority was so important in this organization, partial increases, based upon seniority, had to be granted. Was this a palatable solution for all? The answer was no. If you were a red circle person, you still wanted the entire general increase. If you were not a red circle person, you objected to any increase for those already being paid more than the job was worth. However, because management thought this issue through well in advance and knew that their policy was more generous than that of most other companies, they could defend it as being fair. One of the most important things learned from this issue is that you can do what is best for the business, including making tough decisions that are hard for some to accept, provided that you do it right. Doing it right includes genuine empathy for the effect on the employee, doing all of your homework to see how you compare to industry and area norms, and not putting it into effect until employees and managers have a chance to digest and accept it. All of this is followed by good communication that stresses the *why* as well as the *what*.

Another key step was the establishment of a "pilot group" in the factory who not only tested the revised system but also presented their feelings and concerns to the steering committee. The purpose of the pilot group went well beyond testing the system. The pilot group became a major communication tool and gave management an excellent opportunity to establish its creditability. People learned that management not only listened but when the people were right, took corrective action. Over time, this led to greater openness and trust on the part of everyone involved. The steering committee realized that when introducing major change, this ability to develop openness and trust is essential to achieve the desired results.

Another example shows how empathy, communication, and participation all took place through a well-developed plan. There was a need to establish and build an industrial engineering department to maintain the new system; otherwise, in a few years, all of the old problems would return. A plan was devised to accomplish this. On the surface it seemed to be the long, risky way to go, but in fact it was the most efficient and effective way. It was decided to post the jobs and allow people to bid on the six openings for the new industrial engineering team. Job specifications were carefully written in such a way that factory employees saw they had a chance of meeting the requirements. For example, experience was stressed as being the equivalent or better than a college degree. One goal was to fill as many positions as possible by promotion from the ranks. Another was to be sure that those who were selected would succeed. The position requirements were carefully determined and communicated so that potential candidates could pretty well determine for themselves whether or not they were qualified. They would not even apply if they did not meet the requirements. This was better than having many candidates turned down by management.

Five of the six positions were filled by promotion from the ranks. After extensive training by the consultants, they quickly established their competence. The success of this phase of the change process contributed greatly in reaching the overall goals.

A last crucial decision was whether or not the gains achieved through the productivity improvements brought about by the revised incentive system should be shared with the employees. Here is where the company philosophy determined the way to go. Tremendous stress was placed on seniority, job protection, and the importance of the individual as a member of the family. These fundamental values dictated the decision. If employees were asked to make major contributions to productivity improvements, they had every right to share in the gains. The steering committee realized that if you deny the employees a share of the gains, it would be difficult, if not impossible, to achieve the desired level of productivity improvement. So, it was decided to share the gains with them.

In the middle of all of this dramatic change, a union election was called. The company took an unequivocal position on its desire to stay nonunion. The company firmly believed and practiced a philosophy of one family, one team, as well as that the introduction of a third party would be disruptive and harmful to continued business success. Winning the election became the number one priority and that message was communicated to all. Further, it was made clear to all that the campaign would be fair and honest and that no violations of the labor laws would be tolerated.

After several weeks of hard campaigning, the election was held. The company received 73 percent of the votes and not a single unfair labor practice charge was filed by the union. This would have been a major victory if it had occurred during a quiet period. But coming during a period of tumultuous change, it was an astounding victory. The efforts to improve management's creditability, the honest and open communication, the perception that people were important, the involvement of employees in the change process—all of these things had given the company a firm foundation that not even a union election could shake.

Five years after the changes were introduced, the company's productivity is up 40 percent. The revised incentive system is contributing between $300,000 and $500,000 annually. The vice-president of manufacturing continues to work at communications and continued employee involvement in the decision-making process. For example, a program to involve em-

ployees in determining staffing needs has been successfully in-
augurated. Anticipating that fewer employees would be needed
because of the substantial gain in productivity, the company developed a long-range manpower plan. Through the management
of normal attrition, the company reduced its manufacturing employment by 25 percent and did not lay off a single employee.
Gains were achieved in all areas of manufacturing, and the company not only achieved but even surpassed its desired objectives.

In summation, the company cares about its employees and
expresses that concern on a daily basis. It works hard at maintaining the company values that bind all employees together. It
works hard at determining in advance how people will react to
needed change and it is willing to take time and expend real effort in overcoming their fears and resistance to change. They
communicate regularly so that employees know well in advance
why change is needed, when it will occur, and what its effects
will be. Finally, the company has never lost sight of the im-
mense value of involving people in the change process, from decision making to implementation. It lives the belief that "people are our most important asset." As a result, it has harvested
the rewards that can only come from genuine care, understanding, and willingness to take the time to do things right.

16

ᎳᎳᎳᎳᎳᎳᎳᎳᎳᎳᎳᎳᎳᎳᎳᎳᎳᎳᎳᎳᎳᎳᎳ

Converting from a "Batch" to a "Just-in-Time" Production Process

Currently in America, Japanese management techniques are enjoying particular attention. The most noted of these is the "kanban" or "just-in-time" system. The basic concept is to perform only as much work as required by the customer and only when it is required by the customer.

A division of IBM decided to change from its traditional "batch" manufacturing process to "just-in-time" (JIT). To be successful, the new system required significant changes in tools, procedures, and attitudes of present employees. It would also require extensive training, particularly of new operators. In order to implement the downward communication, the current problems were explained and questions and ideas were solicited. Follow-up meetings were held with those involved to discuss problems and possible solutions. Throughout the decision-making process, input from those involved was asked for, considered, and used. An implementation team was formed to see that the change took place successfully. Key people from the original operations trained the new people. This combination of communication and extensive participation was the key factor in implementing the change with a minimum of problems and a maximum of acceptance.

IBM System Products Division, Rochester, Minnesota
*R. C. Brown, Manager of Test, Instrumentation,
and Software Center
Head Engineering Production Center*

The IBM facility in Rochester, Minnesota has a sizable proportion of its resources devoted to the development and manufacture of all aspects of direct access storage devices (DASD) for the computer industry. One of these aspects has been the manufacture of ferrite heads for hard disk files. Production has been under the control of the Ferrite Head Production Center and has been organized vertically (see Figure 9). The plan was that this organization would inspire greater teamwork between manufacturing, manufacturing engineering, and manufacturing maintenance.

Figure 9. Organization Chart of Ferrite Head Production Center.

Slider Machining	*Head Arm Assembly*	*Business Office*
Manufacturing	Manufacturing	Procurement
Manufacturing Engineering	Manufacturing Engineering	Production Control
		Product Quality
Manufacturing Maintenance	Manufacturing Maintenance	Industrial Engineering
		Plans and Controls

Production control, using the classical batch manufacturing techniques to control the flow of work on the manufacturing floor, issued orders by job lots. As manufacturing engineering began to look at the costs required to increase production capacity, it became obvious that any future expansion would involve extremely high costs due to the long turnaround times of the work-in-process.

It became evident that trying to increase production by pushing batches into the system would result in increased production costs while not necessarily resulting in a direct increase in finished goods. Increased amounts of work-in-process (WIP) would require more production tooling, more floor space for WIP storage, and more direct and indirect manpower to support this tooling and WIP.

In particular, work load and capital plans by the slider machining group indicated that, due to these factors, planned increases in slider volumes would be unaffordable using current manufacturing and production control techniques. As an alternative to the current production management techniques, a method was sought that stressed decreased WIP and turnaround time or pipeline. "Just-in-time" or "kanban" appeared to have these attributes and merit an in-depth study.

Preparation

While several steps were taken to prepare for the JIT study, the first step was communication of the problem to all those involved. To accomplish this, the complete Ferrite Head Production Center (FHPC) staff was brought together and informed of the current business climate and of the steps to be taken to improve its position. In this manner, upper management accomplished three goals:

1. An emphasis on meeting current business goals was directly conveyed to the whole FHPC staff.
2. A willingness to listen to and explore new ideas from all sources was conveyed to the FHPC staff.
3. An active effort was made to build team spirit among all members of the FHPC group.

To further emphasize and build communications and team spirit, meetings were held that involved management, engineers, and manufacturing personnel directly involved with the problem operations. Problems and possible solutions were analyzed in detail. When corrective action was taken, the results were promptly conveyed to the whole team. These steps proved invaluable in optimizing the current manufacturing cycle.

Meanwhile, management was taking steps to become more familiar with the details of JIT manufacturing techniques. Representatives from first-line management attended a detailed seminar on JIT techniques as applied to the complete manufacturing cycle. These representatives then made a detailed report to the complete FHPC management and technical staff. With this understanding of JIT and the manufacturing process, several areas were identified as possible candidates for a JIT pilot program. To further qualify the candidates, a review was made of WIP and finished goods in stock in the various manufacturing areas.

As a result of these activities, the slider machining area was judged most likely to succeed with the JIT approach. The area had a reasonably uncomplicated process flow utilizing one holding fixture—a "nest"—for the major portion of its turnaround time. It also had a significant amount of WIP and a very large inventory of finished goods in stock to serve as a buffer in case of difficulties.

A team, formed with a manufacturing engineer and a manufacturing technician from the slider machining group, was assigned to conduct a detailed assessment of JIT's possibilities in the slider machining area. Their mission was to (1) check feasibility and determine goals for the project, (2) plan and implement JIT, monitoring it closely during initial stages, and (3) report the results to management and the rest of the FHPC.

Implementation

The first questions on everybody's mind were, Is this really possible? How much will it really buy me? To try to answer these questions, a relatively simple simulation program was used that could be customized with the variables pertinent to the current situation. This program quickly demonstrated the benefits of reducing the batch size to one. It showed that the current production requirements could be met while using about one-tenth of the nests and one-tenth of the turnaround time currently required for the process. No significant queues or limitations due to other process machinery were indicated at the current production quantities. Additional cases were simulated to see how many additional nests and what additional process machinery would be required to maintain the desired turnaround time at higher production quantities.

With the indication that significant productivity increases

could be achieved with the currently available resources, the team began developing a plan to implement JIT techniques in the slider machining area. The basic plan was to work the normally required production and "specials" quantities with much less work-in-process. The plan that was developed tried to keep the setting as realistic as possible by working all released product types initially and eventually bringing specials into the line. It also stressed two-way communication in all phases of the trial. This emphasis included initial meetings with all concerned, progress measurement and problem resolution meetings, and finally, meetings to feed results back to manufacturing operators, engineers, and management. Once the plan was reviewed and approved by management, the project began in earnest.

A meeting was held that included management, manufacturing engineers, and manufacturing operators. At this meeting the implementation team explained the JIT concept and the work that had been done to date. The procedures to be used and the responsibilities of both engineers and operators were outlined. The tone of the meeting was one of openness on the part of all. Some of the engineers and operators expressed skepticism and asked questions. Their questions were answered directly and their concerns were treated seriously. Management made clear their understanding that there might be problems getting this system started. They also indicated that they supported the system and wanted to work with the production team to develop management techniques that would be compatible with the new environment.

As the new manufacturing and support procedures were begun, the removal of excess work-in-process (about 240 nests) was perhaps the most traumatic step. The implementation team worked closely with the manufacturing operators during this phase to answer questions and give them support and guidance about new procedures that were to be followed. The implementation team also actively sought suggestions for process improvements from the operators and worked with management, engineers, and other support groups to get them implemented. Where process problems developed, the team established both formal and informal corrective action team meetings with key people from all areas involved and these teams worked to solve the problems. In some cases, one meeting was sufficient to get the problem resolved. In others, however, the teams met regularly for several weeks to develop action plans and solutions. The important feature of these meetings was that the activities and solutions resulted from the combined efforts of all the areas involved.

The implementation team closely monitored production for several months and communicated their findings to operators, engineers, and management. Their data was used to spot process problems in the making and also indicate where progress was being made. The quick and clear feedback of this information to the manufacturing operators seemed to work well, thus enhancing its effectiveness as a problem-solving tool.

After JIT procedures had been in place for several weeks, some fine-tuning and stretching were tried. The WIP that was removed from the manufacturing line was gradually worked back into the line as a filler when normal production jobs weren't available. Heads requiring special processing or "specials" were also tried. In fact, the specials showed a requirement for additional machines in one process and for more detailed process instructions from engineering in several other steps. The inevitable happened. A key inspection machine went down and everybody learned to work together to resolve this critical problem as quickly as possible.

After the people became more accustomed to JIT, it became possible to try some elaborations on the basic procedures. One that was tried was group technology. Group technology allows a bit more flexibility on the manufacturing line in that a number of operators are given responsibility for a group of operators and cross-trained in these operations. While the operators had previously had some cross-training in other processes, the responsibility of a group of operators for a group of operations was stressed much more than before JIT was implemented. In addition, labor and yield claiming and tracking were reduced to one claim at the end of the group of processes instead of a claim after each process. This resulted in a savings of time and labor but there was some loss of detailed information available for process troubleshooting.

Increasing quantities became necessary and new operators were needed to be selected and trained. Both of these changes were handled relatively smoothly because of the planning by the implementation team and the familiarity of the operators with the JIT techniques. Initially the introduction of more nests or process tools into the process was handled by the original operators with only minimal overtime. While some changes to process machinery were required, they were accomplished smoothly through close cooperation between the engineers and operators.

As the quantities increased even further, a second and third shift were added. Key people from the original operators trained the new people required to staff these shifts. The biggest problems encountered in this expansion were the implementation team trying to cover and monitor production on three unbalanced shifts. However, recording and monitoring procedures were quickly standardized and taught to the manufacturing technicians. This eventually freed the implementation team so they could look for additional steps that could be taken to further improve the process flow.

Results

As the just-in-time techniques became the accepted way of doing business in slider machining, the results became more evident in areas such as manufacturing costs, product quality, and employee morale.

The most obvious change to the manufacturing process also resulted in the most obvious cost savings. The number of in-process nests was cut from 260 to 21. This reduced in-process product inventory and tooling costs. This change also reduced the manufacturing pipeline for the next operations in the slider machining area from ten days to one day. Another improvement in this area was a reduction in direct man-hours required. These immediate improvements significantly lowered costs in all the areas just mentioned when production quantities were increased.

Quality remained high throughout the study period. The reduction of in-process buffers was one of the key factors that allowed this to happen. The operators were able to catch problems earlier through both formal and informal communication channels because they knew exactly where the parts they were working on came from—buffers didn't get in the way and confuse things. With less in-process buffer stock, the yield numbers reported were much more representative of the current line status and also allowed much quicker response to problems by support personnel.

Although operators, engineers, and management were somewhat skeptical at first, as the results began to come in they supported the program and worked enthusiastically for its success. Taking the case of group technology as an example, the operators have responded well to the increased responsibility and the new variety in their jobs. The engineers have begun to include the operators in initial design reviews for new equipment and processes. Management has developed new ways to measure operator performance that are more suited to the just-in-time environment and group technology situations. This teamwork and close communication between the groups has been a positive result, encouraging the continued use of just-in-time in slider machining and the extension of these techniques to the head arm assembly area.

Summary

The conversion from batch to just-in-time techniques in the slider machining area brought many changes to the accepted way of doing business (see Table 4).

Good communication and involvement at all levels were the most important factors in the success of this conversion. While providing direction and emphasis to the employee, management's willingness to listen and react promptly to the employees' concerns and questions played a large part in the success of this project. The close interaction between engineering,

Table 4. Comparisons Between Batch and Just-In-Time.

Batch	Just-In-Time
Push inventory through line	Pull inventory through line
Large job lots	Small job lots (single unit)
Much of work-in-process (260 nests)	Minimal work-in-process (21 nests)
Long in-process pipeline (ten days average in nests)	Short in-process pipeline (one day average in nests)
Manufacturing engineering and maintenance fixed problems	All groups work together to solve problems; operators do simple maintenance
Problems hidden in buffers and solved only when a crisis arose	Problems solved immediately to keep the line running
Causes of problems forgotten in passing of time	Details surrounding problems still fresh in everyone's mind

operations, and maintenance allowed process and equipment changes to be made rapidly in ways that were acceptable to all. This continuous two-way communication between managers, engineers, operators, and maintenance people built team spirit, minimized problems and defects, and made this dramatic change successful.

17

Reorganizing
the Sales Force

Because of changing market needs, new product development, and increased competition, many organizations have changed the way in which they sell their products. One such change was planned and implemented at Xerox Corporation. It was successful because of a combination of complete and open communication and extensive participation in the form of task teams.

Xerox Corporation, El Segundo, California
W. W. Castor, Senior Vice-President
Xerox Systems Marketing Division

In early 1982, it became apparent that two major trends were occurring in the office systems marketplace. The first dealt with the customer environment and the second with the direction of the product technologies of Xerox. The logical impact of these two trends mandated a major shift in the way Xerox sold its products. This shift would necessitate a strategic change in the cultural selling patterns of the company. In addition, it was important to alter the company's long-term selling patterns without disrupting the day-to-day business activities of the company.

In 1982, the Xerox marketplace essentially consisted of two general business areas. One was driven by the traditional business base of copiers and duplicating equipment, the other by several different product lines in the office systems and electronic printing business. The latter is referred to within Xerox as the "systems business." These two business areas had been represented to the marketplace with over seven different sales forces. Past endeavors to coordinate these selling efforts within large accounts, through the use of a major account sales force, had met with marginal success. Indeed, several Xerox accounts had requested "one face" to work with in terms of support, service, administration, and contracting. It was anticipated that these concerns would grow, especially because the customer environment itself was changing.

Changing Customer Environments

Most large organizations are faced with combining and coordinating new office automation systems with the somewhat more deeply rooted operations common to data processing departments. In the face of an exponential growth of information, it becomes especially important to organize a central point to plan and implement a company-wide system of information distribution and exchange. Indeed, the productivity of the so-called knowledge worker is critically dependent on the worker having the latest information relative to his or her field. In addition, the proliferation of personal computers at modest prices has encouraged a helter-skelter buying of these products that, unfortunately, often cannot communicate with one another or with other office automation equipment. The result is that there will continue to be major pressures on organizations to centralize the responsibility for their total office and information systems needs.

In turn, this means vendor companies with diverse product lines in the information systems and office systems business must deal with customers in a highly coordinated fashion. Specifically, vendors must present "one face" to customers in order to meet their needs for an integrated system of information distribution. Furthermore, vendors will have to look upon their current and future product lines with an eye toward integrating and complimenting their functionality for added value to a customer's total system.

The new environments at customer locations could best be met, in the view of Xerox, by merging office automation technologies. For example, the flow of Xerox products at a customer site generally involved electronic printers accepting information from the host computers and then distributing this same information to headquarters and field locations. Xerox work stations, professional computers, word processors, facsimile transmission devices, and scanners could all be linked to a local area network. Remote printers, in the early 1980s, were beginning to have local copying capabilities, and the future distinctions of product functions were seen to be merging.

By 1982, it was clear what customers would be doing, what Xerox products would be doing, and, most important, what Xerox had to do with its diverse sales forces. What was not clear, however, was how to integrate separate sales forces and separate selling cultures to meet customer needs without disrupting ongoing business activities.

Planning for Change

The first and most important decision to be made upon resolving to integrate the selling forces of Xerox was whether to do the planning in an open forum or in secrecy. Experiences noted in other corporations indicated that planning in secrecy avoided the perceived risks of eroding employee attitudes toward their job stability. Planning for this change in an open forum could result in loss of productivity and loss of employees. Moreover, secretive planning would avoid a drawn-out abrasion and result, it is hoped, in a short and sudden shock when it was all announced. But there were two major drawbacks in planning this sales integration action in secret. First, there would be limited input on ideas for implementing the change and, second, limited commitment to its successful implementation. The option of planning major organization changes in an open forum had not been tried very often in other large corporations. Apparently, it had not been tried because of these risks. Nevertheless, there were many strong arguments for planning this change in an open forum. For instance, the diversity of internal organizations selling Xerox products meant that an excellent opportunity existed for ideas to be shared. Also, the need for employee commitment to an integrated sales force was vitally important. Xerox had been successful in previous internal reorganizations by getting employees involved. And, equally important, it was felt that by planning for an integrated sales force in an open forum, there would be less employee apprehension than if it were done in secret.

In September of 1982, David Kearns, the president of Xerox, made the first internal announcement of the intent to integrate the selling forces of Xerox. The announcement explained the rationale for this restructuring and described the process by which it would be accomplished. The process would involve a task team composed of members from the various sales organizations. These people would solicit input from ongoing employee involvement groups and there would be a steady stream of correspondence to keep all employees informed.

The communication from Mr. Kearns was a bold and forthright move. It expressed the need for the involvement of all employees and, thereby, conveyed the importance of employees to the company. All key managers within Xerox were briefed prior to the announcement to allow a closely coordinated response to employee questions and to be more sensitive to their reactions. The communications were successful in avoiding negative reactions and in building a positive commitment to the job ahead.

Achieving Objectives

The processes employed to achieve objectives involved three phases: the planning phase, which would consider various options and the anticipated effects; the evaluation phase, to allow a reasonable testing of key alternatives; and the implementation phase.

The planning phase was orchestrated by a full-time task team of representatives from each of the major sales organizations. This team reported to an executive steering committee that included group-level executives and was chaired by the executive vice-president of Xerox. The task team made full use of employee involvement teams. The employee involvement teams could be dynamically structured at any time to address key issues during the planning phase. The task team would formally report progress and issues to be resolved to the steering committee on a monthly schedule. Communications to employees were continued at all levels. There was an open-door environment to individual employees who had questions of personal concern. Indeed, the planning phase resulted in a scenario of several key alternative implementation structures for integrating the separate sales forces into a more focused response to customer buying requirements.

The evaluation phase consisted of structuring trial implementations of three key alternatives, with three locations selected. The local organizations were asked to take an active role in structuring the best way of evaluating their specific alternative approach. Consistent measurement criteria were established for the locations. Individual members of the task team were assigned to each of the three locations to act as facilitators, observers, and recorders. The level of commitment that resulted from the three trial locations not only exceeded the level of expectations but became a very competitive environment. Each location was bent on being the best in terms of meeting their business objectives, a most welcome result. Based upon the final evaluation of trials over an eight-month period, a decision was made for what represented the most effective sales organization structure. Again, results were quickly communicated to all employees.

The implementation phase began by shifting control from a task team to a set of key line managers representing the major organization elements involved. To help communicate the implementation phase to employees, a videotape was developed. It presented the plan, its rationale, structure, and the time frame of the phasing process. The presenters in the videotape were the key line managers. This allowed a personal identification with the leadership of the various organizations, demonstrated their interest and commitment to the task at hand, and conveyed assurances that there would be definite benefits to all employees in terms of greater career opportunities.

A large part of this message was in the medium itself. Much time and care went into a highly professional production. The result was a positive reaction from employees in that the company cared about them as individuals and as key members of the new organization.

During the more than two years it took to complete the various phases, sales and profits grew very close to the business plan. In several organizations, performance and profits significantly exceeded plan. Moreover, there was no substantial increase in employee turnover. And in terms of customer impact, the entire process was transparent to them. There were no registered customer complaints of being neglected due to organization change. Many customers, in fact, expressed their satisfaction with the extra attention given their accounts.

Conclusions

The conclusion we reached from this experience is that major company reorganizations can best be achieved in an open communications environment. Employee involvement is mandatory. Rather than encountering the risks of disruption and long-term employee abrasion, Xerox fostered an atmosphere of trust, participation, and employee security. The vehicles to accomplish this may be summarized as follows:

- Senior executive commitment to the objectives and to the process.
- Open and complete communications to all employees through a variety of communication vehicles on a continuing basis. Communication is not an event. It is a process.
- Solicitation and use of employee input through problemsolving circles or through any other vehicle an employee desires to communicate ideas and concerns. All employee input must be welcomed with equal respect and response.
- Reinforcement of the process to all employees. Acknowledgment of valued input must be related and commended publicly to achieve ownership of the final plan.

Xerox believes the long-term implications of the success of this endeavor will reap large rewards in terms of customer satisfaction, employee productivity, and general business results. The corporation intends to maintain a continued follow-up and evaluation for further enhancing the new structure and ensuring employee involvement.

18

◯I◯I◯I◯I◯I◯I◯I◯I◯I◯I◯I◯I◯I◯I◯I◯I◯I◯I◯I◯I◯I◯I◯I◯I◯

Instituting
New Training Programs

Recognizing the need for training and development and doing it are two different things. This case describes the inception and growth of a comprehensive training program in a large hospital. One of the significant changes was the establishment of one training department that included nurses' training, which had previously reported to the director of nursing. A combination of empathy, communication, and participation made the change successful.

A Large Boston Hospital
Dr. Edward E. Jones, President
Management Training Consultants, Wakefield, Rhode Island

A large Boston-based teaching hospital was uncertain of its level of management expertise. There were no means in place to evaluate effectiveness. No hospital-based management skills development and training existed. Only in-service technical education for nurses took place. Nonnursing managers comprised three quarters of the management staff. These individuals took courses, seminars, and programs with no guidance or direction from the hospital administration.

The need for a concerted training and development effort was recognized in late 1979. Top-level administrators knew that they were responsible for training their management personnel with the hospital's overall goals in mind. They recognized that better management would result in better patient services. The executives felt that managers were responsible for training and developing their staff on policy and procedures of the hospital as well as good management practices. They recognized that this need was not being met by a systematic and unified approach. Another driving force for additional training was stepped-up union activity. At the time, the only group organized was the nurses. Based on these factors, the vice-president of human resources was given the assignment to actively pursue possible approaches for the training and development of all three levels of management within the hospital.

Not all the top administrators totally supported the idea of a formal approach to training and development. Some felt it was a waste of money and took staff away from their assigned work stations without producing tangible results. Therefore, a cost/benefit analysis was undertaken. This was done by comparing all costs related to sending staff to outside sources with the proposals submitted by outside consultants for in-house training. In addition, it was pointed out that in-house management education could be directed more specifically to the management difficulties and styles unique to the hospital. Finally, discussions by the president and executive vice-president strongly reinforced in-house education and helped persuade other managers to agree. As a result, the eight top executives agreed to hire an outside consulting firm to give management training to all three levels of managers. After the initial approval, the vice-president of human resources continuously reinforced training and development in the administrative meetings by stressing the benefits of such programs with concrete examples of improved quality in interviewing and selection of personnel and better utilization of performance appraisals to maximize the human resources' potential available in the hospital.

One hundred twenty-five managers began the required program in basic management skill development. Some managers welcomed the opportunity for growth while others resisted, saying they din't have time. A third group remained neutral. For many of the managers, the learning that was occurring was immediately being implemented back on the job. The positive results of the program were reinforced through the internal newsletter and administrative memos from the president and executive vice-president. As managers continued to benefit from the training, they began to pressure top administration for more programs for themselves as well as in-house education for their staff, believing it would be cost-effective in terms of both money and time. Based on these pressures, the executives determined there was a need for a full-time education function at the hospital.

In late 1980 a training director was hired and the groundwork for change had been laid. The director's job was to emphasize the need and create meaningful educational programs to help reach the hospital's short- and long-term objectives. A training and development department was established. While the nursing division had seven instructors and a director, the new training director was the only person assigned to management, personal growth, affirmative action, and adult education training. As a first step, the new director ensured continued basic management skills training by making the training a required part of the general hospital orientation program for all new managers.

The director conducted a needs analysis, using interviews

with selected management personnel and questionnaires to managers and nonmanagement staff. Hospital reports were also read. Some programs, such as programs dealing with affirmative action, were mandated by external influences. The community that the hospital served had changed in racial and ethnic makeup while the hospital had not changed its makeup or response to the community.

After attending popular programs such as "Time Management," "Conducting Effective Meetings," and "English as a Second Language," hospital personnel were asking for other programs. Effective program design and leadership resulted in more and more enthusiasm from those who attended. After each program, whether a half-day, full-day, or twelve-week program, participants enthusiastically talked with others about the learning that had occurred. This excitement and learning convinced others of the value of the programs. Suggestions for program development were increased and prioritized in accordance with the hospital's goals. Requests to participate were handled on a first-come, first-served basis.

By the end of 1981, there were more and more demands for training and development. With this increased desire, it was time to make the first of many changes in the staff development department, namely, to hire additional staff. At this time the director had a secretary and had periodically hired two outside consultants to do in-house workshops. Hospital administration was asked to approve a proposal for hiring two additional trainers and to develop a training center.

An innovative approach to training in a hospital, that of a separate training facility that could be a self-supporting cost center, was recommended to top management by the training director. Extensive financial analysis had proved that effective training could be done for approximately two dollars per staff member. Discussions also centered on getting maximum use of the training facility by marketing the programs to outside organizations. A building a block away from the hospital was rented and remodeled. Because participants attended sessions away from the work site, it gave the training function increased credibility in the minds of those participating.

To staff this facility and the continuously increasing needs for staff education, two additional trainers were considered. While these two were professional trainers, they represented a significant change in hospital hiring practice because neither had any hospital experience. Resistance to this change was overcome by inviting the trainers to present brief programs to managers before they were hired. Because they were qualified and also because of this participative approach, management support was ensured.

After the training department had been expanded, the question of having two training departments—one for nursing and one for management training—surfaced. Managers questioned the cost justification of separate departments. At the same time, the director of nursing education resigned. The position was kept vacant for six months during which time the vice-presidents asked such questions as: Was it necessary to fill the position? Should the two education departments be merged? If so, what are the benefits? What are the drawbacks?

After extensive study, it was decided that it was better to have one department. An informal committee made up of the vice-president for human resources, vice-president for nursing, three nursing directors, and the training director spent much time convincing key people in the nursing division that it wouldn't lose its educational arm but would benefit from the merger. After weighing the advantages and disadvantages at numerous discussions, the vice-president for nursing agreed that it would be in the best interest of the hospital and all parties to merge. By merging, nursing gave up direct fiscal and administrative control of education. A nursing educational committee was set up to identify nursing education needs and to offer suggestions on how to meet those needs. This committee was instituted to be sure that the hospital-wide education department paid special attention to the learning needs of nursing personnel.

In addition to identifying technical educational nursing needs, the nursing educational committee was also responsible for identifying other nursing educational needs. Management courses were developed on such subjects as leadership, motivation, stress management, and affirmative action.

Summary

The development of a hospital-wide education department was a drastic change. From the beginning, feelings were divided. Some people at all levels favored it while others were strongly opposed. Others could care less, as long as they received the training and development they desired. The creation of a hospital-wide education department proved to be a success. Employees' educational needs were being met; cost reduction had been achieved by consolidation of the departments; and those individuals fearful of the change accepted the department and its efforts because of the success the department had in meeting the entire hospital's educational needs.

During the process of deciding on the changes and getting them implemented successfully, questions like the following were raised:

- Who will oppose the change and how strongly do they feel?
- Who is supporting the change and how powerful are they?
- How much will the change cost?
- What benefits will be derived?
- How and when should the proposed changes be communicated?
- What are the best ways to get key people to participate in the change?

The answers to these questions are related to the three keys stressed in this book—empathy, communication, and participation. The effective implementation of these changes resulted from a careful study of each question as well as carefully determined answers that were tailor-made to this specific hospital.

Summary:
How to Be an Effective
Change Manager

Managing change can be the most important and satisfying thing you do as a manager. It offers possibilities for improving the effectiveness of your department and organization. It can bring about a quality of work life with its improvement of personal satisfaction and morale on the part of your subordinates. It can result in both nonmonetary and monetary rewards for you, the manager.

This book has described the roles that you should play as a manager, as follows:

- *Implement changes from above.* If you are in favor of them, do it enthusiastically. If you think the changes are a mistake, challenge your boss by telling him/her how you feel and give your reasons. Suggest an alternative approach. But if your boss insists you carry it out, do so with as much enthusiasm as possible.
- *Decide on changes that you think should be made.* When you do this, you have two choices: (1) recommend the change to your boss and ask for approval, or (2) initiate the change without asking your boss for approval.

  Each of these choices presents a risk. If you recommend, you are taking a risk that the boss might say, "No!

255

You can't do it!" If you initiate it without asking for approval, you are risking the anger of your boss who feels that you should recommend rather than initiate.

The solution is to understand your boss well enough to know how much authority you have.

Chapter Three presents philosophy and recommendations from various authors. Although their approaches are different, the common theme is to know your people, communicate completely, and get them involved in the change process. A model for planning and implementing change is presented in Chapter Five.

Chapters Six, Seven, and Eight constitute the heart of the book. They describe what to do and how to do it. Specific suggestions are provided to implement the three keys for managing change—empathy, communication, and participation.

Empathy

- Know your people.
- Know why some people resent/resist change while others accept/welcome it (Chapter Four).
- Anticipate how each person affected will react to a contemplated change.

Communication

- Let people know as far in advance as practical.
- Provide the reasons "why" as well as the "what" and the "how."
- Be sure they understand.

Participation

- Before a decision to change is final, get input from those involved.
- Listen to them and carefully consider their opinions as well as the facts.
- To the extent possible, use their input in making the decision.

- If their input is not used, be sure to tell them why it wasn't used.
- Give them credit.

The case studies illustrate how a number of organizations have managed change effectively. They were careful to make the right decisions on what changes to make. Equally important, they were able to get maximum acceptance when implementing the change.

These are the two challenges you face as a manager of change: What changes should be made? How can you get maximum acceptance from those who are involved?

It is hoped that this book has provided you with philosophy, principles, and techniques to answer these questions. As was stated in the preface, the contents of this book have provided you with the "science" of management—organized knowledge. The "art" of management is up to you—the application of this knowledge to your own particular situation to accomplish the desired, practical results.

One final word. Before you put the book aside, complete the Posttest on the following pages. Compare your responses with mine. Compare them with your Pretest responses. Did you learn anything? Are there items where you and I have different answers? If yes, you may want to reread parts of the book. Or, you may want to say, "I understand why we differ. In my situation my answer is better." And that is O.K. too, because my objective has been accomplished: to provide you with the "science" of management—organized knowledge of concepts, theories, principles, and techniques. Your objective has also been accomplished: to use the "art" of management—the application to your own particular situation to accomplish desired, practical results.

So, may you be successful in managing changes that face you, now and in the future.

ଠାଠ

Posttest:
A Self-Assessment
of Change Management
Knowledge

Insert *A* (agree) or *D* (disagree) in front of each question to indicate your opinion.

———— 1. Your boss has decided on a change that you feel would be a mistake. You should go ahead and implement it without challenging it.

———— 2. Managers should constantly be looking for changes that will improve department efficiency and/or morale.

———— 3. If you were promoted to a management job, you should make the job different than it was under your predecessor.

———— 4. "You can't argue with success."

———— 5. People doing a particular job are one of the best sources of ideas to improve that job.

———— 6. Very few people in any department have any ideas to improve the effectiveness of the department or the organization.

———— 7. In order to get a large number of suggestions from people, you must give money or prizes for ideas that are accepted and implemented.

_____ 8. Managers should freely suggest changes to managers in other departments.

_____ 9. Most managers would welcome ideas and suggestions from people in other departments.

_____ 10. Managers should welcome ideas and suggestions from all sources.

_____ 11. If you think a change should be made in your department, you should always ask your boss for approval before making the change.

_____ 12. If changes do not have any impact on other departments, you should implement the changes without bothering to clear them with your boss.

_____ 13. If a change doesn't cost any money, you should implement it without bothering to clear it with your boss.

_____ 14. The style of leadership of the boss is the most important factor to consider when managers are trying to decide whether to recommend or initiate a change.

_____ 15. Bosses and subordinates should have an understanding regarding the kinds of changes that can be implemented by the subordinate without getting prior approval from the boss.

_____ 16. You should encourage your subordinates to try out any changes that they feel should be made.

_____ 17. If your boss says no to a change you've recommended, you should forget about it.

_____ 18. The quality of a decision based on facts and logic is more important than the acceptance of those who must carry it out.

_____ 19. Changes based on facts and logic can be sabotaged, intentionally or not, by persons affected by the change.

_____ 20. If you are planning to make a radical change in your department, you should secretly gather facts, prepare your final plans, and sell those people affected on the basis of facts and logic.

_____ 21. In order to save time and be decisive, a manager

should make decisions regarding change without seeking input from subordinates.

_____ 22. Decisions to change should be based on opinions as well as facts.

_____ 23. Managers should always maintain the authority to make the final decision when they ask for input from subordinates.

_____ 24. If subordinates participate in the decision to make a change, they are usually more enthusiastic in carrying it out.

_____ 25. If a change has been implemented and it isn't working out as expected, the change should be rescinded and the old way should be reinstated.

_____ 26. You've decided on a change and announced it. You then receive more data and now know it's a mistake. You should retract the decision and apologize for the mistake.

_____ 27. When you've decided on a change and announced it to your subordinates, you should never retract it even if it is not well received.

_____ 28. People with negative attitudes toward change should be encouraged to quit.

_____ 29. If one subordinate enthusiastically resists a change, you should clamp down hard on that person so the other subordinates won't do the same thing.

_____ 30. People will automatically accept changes decided on by experts.

_____ 31. You should tell your subordinates as far in advance as practical about a change that will affect them.

_____ 32. People should be informed in advance of unpleasant changes as well as pleasant changes.

_____ 33. If a change is going to be resisted no matter what you do, there is no point in communicating the reasons for the change.

_____ 34. If a change is going to result in the termination of one or more people, this should be made clear before the change is implemented.

_____ 35. You should do everything you can to find other jobs for people whose jobs are eliminated by a change.

_____ 36. It's a good idea to sell a change to the natural leader among your subordinates before trying to sell it to the others.

_____ 37. It is usually better to communicate with a group concerning a change than to talk to each person individually.

_____ 38. Explaining the reasons for a change will always turn resistance into acceptance.

_____ 39. Logical explanation by a manager will not be accepted if the feelings of the subordinates are ignored.

_____ 40. If a change is introduced at the right time, by the right person, in the right manner, it will always be accepted.

_____ 41. People who don't understand the reasons for a change will always resist it.

_____ 42. People are always anxious to move from an old office to a new one.

_____ 43. People are always anxious to have new equipment to work with.

_____ 44. Some people are not anxious to be promoted to a job with more responsibility.

_____ 45. One of the most frequent reasons why employees resent and/or resist change is the fear they might lose something.

_____ 46. The timing of a change can be very important in its acceptance.

_____ 47. Before making a change, managers should determine to what extent subordinates will accept the change.

_____ 48. Once you've decided on a change, you should implement it immediately.

_____ 49. Most people will accept a change if managers explain that the change is necessary for the survival of the organization.

_____ 50. When a change has been decided on, it is a good
idea to get subordinates involved in helping you
implement the change.

Answers
to Pretest and Posttest

D   1.   The word *challenge* needs to be defined because many bosses don't like to be challenged. It consists of three steps: Give the boss your opinion, tell him/her why you think it's a mistake, and offer your recommendation. Obviously, it should be done in a tactful manner.

A   2.   The word *constantly* may be a little strong but it emphasizes that managers should do more than maintain the status quo until the boss says, "Change!"

A   3.   Most managers will mark this item *D* because they read into it that the changes should be immediate and drastic. They also feel it implies "change for change sake," even if things are O.K. as is. In other words, "If it ain't broke, don't fix it!" It was not intended to imply that drastic changes should be made immediately. Rather, the rationale for "agree" is that all jobs can be improved. We can argue with success. And each person who moves into a higher-level job should make changes that can improve productivity as well as morale.

D   4.   This is one of the reasons for the answer to item 3.

A   5. They have firsthand knowledge of job problems and will probably have ideas for solving the problems as well as for doing the job in a more efficient manner.

D   6. The success of participative management teams (quality circles, and so on) has proved over and over again that practically everyone has ideas for improving the effectiveness of an organization. Managers must give them the opportunity and encouragement to express these ideas freely.

D   7. Some organizations have been very successful with suggestion systems that pay for ideas that are used. They are able to generate many ideas they wouldn't have received without the system. This doesn't mean, however, that it is the only solution. Managers can also stimulate ideas by maintaining rapport with subordinates, encouraging suggestions, implementing and giving credit for those that are used, and explaining why others were not used. Employees will continue to offer suggestions to these managers, whether on an individual basis or through work teams.

A or D 8. The answer to this question depends to a large extent on the answer to item 9. The answer to both questions should be the same because they are closely related. If, for example, managers would not welcome ideas and suggestions, then it would be a waste of time to suggest them.

A or D 9. I trust you have the right answer for your organization.

A   10. The difference between this question and item 9 is *should* versus *would*. Managers *should* welcome suggestions from all sources. They might not accept and use all of them, but they should encourage them.

D   11. The better answer is probably *D* because of the word *always*. Whether to ask for approval each time depends on four principal factors: the size of the change, the cost, whether or not it will affect other departments, and the leadership style of the boss in regard to decision making. If the style of the boss is that he/she makes *all* the decisions and subordinates simply recommend, the answer to this item is *A*. But in nearly all cases, subordinates are able to make minor changes without clearing them with the boss.

A or D   12.   Either answer is correct, depending on other factors including the style of leadership of your boss.

A or D   13.   Same as 12.

A   14.   This has been emphasized in item 11.

A   15.   This is important in order to let subordinates know when to initiate and when to go to the boss for approval.

A or D   16.   In most cases the *DA* answer is probably best because of possible mistakes that could be costly in terms of quantity, scrap, or even accidents. It is probably best to have subordinates suggest ideas rather than to give them the authority to make changes on their own. There are cases, however, where capable and reliable subordinates should be given the freedom to act without first checking with the supervisor.

D   17.   Managers can learn a lesson from salespeople. If the customer says no, the salesperson doesn't say O.K. and forget it. He or she usually plans another call and picks a better time, uses a different approach, or does something else that is different than the first try. The typical salesperson calls on new customers an average of five times before making the first sale. Likewise, managers should not take no for a final answer if they feel their idea has merit.

D   18.   Good decisions can fail because of the lack of acceptance on the part of those who must implement them. Employees who don't like a decision may resent it (an attitude) or resist it (an action). And they have usually learned how to do it in a subtle way so it isn't out-and-out sabotage. Rather, they will quietly see to it that it doesn't work out. One of the reasons why participative management is so popular is because it not only provides practical ideas but also results in commitment on the part of those who helped make the decision.

A   19.   This is the main reason for the *D* answer to item 18.

D   20.   Although this approach is sometimes successful, there are two other approaches that will usually result in better decisions and stronger acceptance. The first approach is to get input from those involved from the very beginning. Their thoughts and suggestions should be carefully considered in making the final decision and also in getting the plan implemented. The second approach is for managers to make one or more *tentative* plans and get reactions from those involved. Managers who use the last approach should be very careful that they don't become defensive when subordinates "attack" their plan. Managers must be willing to change the plan if input from subordinates warrants. They must even be willing to throw out their plans and start over. If they defend their tentative plan, subordinates are apt to get the message that the boss has already decided and input from subordinates will not be considered. This will cut off upward communication.

A or D 21.   Yes, a manager can save time initially and be decisive without seeking input from subordinates. However, this may result in a decision that is resisted by them and *doesn't work out,* and much time will be needed in the future to overcome the resistance or change the decision.

A   22.   Traditional approaches to problem solving emphasized "get the facts." And managers were urged to differentiate between facts and opinions. Peter Drucker (1967) says that executives should encourage opinions. He states that if you ask for facts, you will only get those facts that fit the conclusion they have already reached. Therefore, opinions can help managers make the best decisions. Another reason for getting opinions is to build acceptance and even commitment on the part of those who have participated.

D   23.   The word *always* is too strong. There are two ways to make decisions that include input from subordinates. One is to ask for opinions, facts, ideas, and so on and reserve the authority to make the decision. The second approach is to use the group problem-solving approach in which the manager leads the subordinates to a group decision. There are advantages and disadvantages of each approach.

A   24.   This is especially true if the decision is made by the group or if the manager uses their input in making the decision. It is also true if the subordinates feel that their input has been carefully considered, even if the decision is not what they suggested. In this situation, a manager must explain why their input was not used.

D   25.   This answer simply means "not necessarily." Other alternative actions are to modify the decision or to gain acceptance by moving more slowly than planned.

A   26.   Some managers object to the word *apologize.* They feel it is not a good idea to do this. They fail to realize that an apology usually gains respect when people know that a mistake has been made. Many managers who agree with the statement find it difficult to do because pride is involved.

D   27.   The word *never,* of course, makes this a disagree item. There are times when it is a good idea to retract it and apologize as described in item 26. If you still think the decision is a good one, then it is best to try to persuade those who resist it that it is a good decision.

D   28.   One foreman who answered "disagree" had this reason: "We shouldn't encourage them to quit; we ought to *fire them!*" Perhaps this is good advice as a last resort, but the first approach is to determine the reason for the negative attitude and try to change it.

D   29.   Usually this approach will backfire and other employees will resent what the manager did to one of their co-workers. This approach may be best if the person is an obvious troublemaker who is trying to see how far he/she can go in challenging the authority of the manager. In this situation, other employees will probably support the action.

D   30.   It makes little difference who decides on a change if it is going to have a negative effect, such as personal loss to employees.

A   31.   One of the most difficult decisions for a manager is the timing of the announcement of a change. If it will have a positive effect, it should be done at a time to get maximum benefit. If it will have a negative effect on employees, the timing depends on the rapport that has been developed between the manager and subordinates. If employees will be upset and damage equipment or take similar action, it is best to wait until the last minute. However, if employees will appreciate the fact that the manager told them in advance so they could adjust to it, then it should be communicated earlier. The key word is *practical,* which means that various factors should be considered.

A   32. A manager—and the entire organization—should build a reputation for communicating to employees when decisions are made. The exception would be the situation described in the answer to item 31 in which employees would take destructive action.

D   33. It is important to communicate the "why" as well as the "what" and "when" of such a change. A company should build a reputation for doing this, even if the decision will not be popular.

A   34. As stated in previous statements, honesty is the best policy and the impact of the change should be explained. If it comes as a surprise later on, the employees will be more upset than if they had been forewarned.

A   35. This ties in with item 34. If people are going to lose jobs, the company should not only inform them of the reasons for the change but also do whatever is possible to find jobs for those who will be terminated. This will build positive attitudes on the part of all employees whether terminated or not.

A   36. By definition, a "natural leader" is a person that other employees look to for advice and counsel. If this person is sold on the change, it will help to gain acceptance on the part of the others.

A or D   37. There are advantages and disadvantages to each approach. When the group approach is used, everyone gets the same story at the same time. There is no suspicion regarding what the manager tells each employee. Also, there is no opportunity for the grapevine to operate. It can be risky if there is enough resistance to stir up the whole crowd. The individual approach has the advantage of tailoring the explanation to each person. The manager can explain the benefits to each person. Also, it is probably easier to get comments and questions from each individual.

The disadvantage is the suspicion that different people are told different stories and the grapevine will pick up the information and pass it around before some employees hear it firsthand. In either case it is a good idea to be sure that the natural leader is in favor of the change.

D   38.   Logic and reasons for a change may not turn resistance into acceptance if the individual is going to lose something in the process.

A   39.   This is related to item 38. If people fear they will lose something by the change, their feelings and emotions will be strong. Logical explanation will usually be ineffective in changing resistance to acceptance.

D   40.   This is similar to item 30. If employees are going to lose something by the change, the conditions under which it is introduced will probably have no effect.

D   41.   The key factor is whether people will gain or lose from the change. People who will gain money, security, status, authority, or better working conditions won't be very concerned with the reasons for the change. They will be primarily concerned with how it will affect them.

D   42.   Some new offices are smaller, less private, and less comfortable than old offices.

D   43.   Sometimes, new equipment will take effort to learn to operate, will be more difficult to use, and will create a feeling of insecurity on the part of the employee.

A   44.   Some people simply don't want more responsibility either because they are happy with what they are doing or because they are afraid they will not be able to handle it.

A   45.   Some of the things they fear are loss of job, money, status, authority, responsibility, visibility, and a feeling of achievement.

A   46.   Acceptance can be a matter of timing. If, for

example, a change that creates problems is presented to a person who is already having problems, it will be resisted. On the other hand, if a change that will save money is presented when a person is under pressure to cut expenses, it will be welcomed.

A 47. This is one of the most important principles and one of the three keys to managing change. Empathy for those involved is necessary in order to know what changes to make and how best to implement them.

D 48. Not necessarily. The speed with which it is introduced should be related to the amount of resistance. If everyone is in favor of it, don't wait. If, however, resistance is high, it should be introduced slowly.

A or D 49. It depends on the credibility and rapport that has been established in the organization.

A 50. Sometimes changes are decided on without getting input from subordinates. Sometimes input is obtained and considered before making a decision to change. In either case, input in implementing the change is a good idea because of the high degree of acceptance it will obtain.

References

Behavioral Sciences Newsletter, Mahway, N.J., September 27, 1983a.

Behavioral Sciences Newsletter, Mahwah, N.J., October 24, 1983b, p. 3.

Bennett, T. R. III. *Planning for Change.* Washington, D.C.: Leadership Resources, 1961.

Blake, R., and Mouton, J. S. *Productivity: The Human Side.* New York: Amacom, 1982.

Buckley, K. W., and Perkins, D. *Managing the Complexity of Organizational Transformation.* Alexandria, Va.: Miles River Press, 1984.

Burack, E. H., and Torda, F. *The Manager's Guide to Change.* Lake Forest, Ill.: Brace-Park Press, 1979.

Coch, L., and French, J. R. P., Jr. "Overcoming Resistance to Change." *Human Relations,* 1948, *1* (4).

Conner, D. R., and Patterson, R. *Building Commitment to Organizational Change.* Atlanta: O.D. Resources, 1981.

Drucker, P. F. *The Effective Executive.* New York: Harper & Row, 1967.

Geiger, Z. U. "Be Worthy of Your Hire!" Mt. Cory Carriage and Wagon Works, April 5, 1872.

Hersey, P., and Blanchard, K. H. "The Management of Change." *Training and Development Journal,* January 1972.

Ingle, S. "Implementing Quality Circles." Rockville, Md.: BNA Communications, 1982.

Ingle, S. *Quality Circles Master Guide.* Englewood Cliffs, N.J.: Prentice-Hall, 1982b.

Ingle, S., and Ingle, M. *Quality Circles in Service Industries.* Englewood Cliffs, N.J.: Prentice-Hall, 1983.

Kanter, R. M. *The Change Masters.* New York: Simon and Schuster, 1983.

Kirkpatrick, D. L. *How to Improve Performance Through Appraisal and Coaching.* New York: Amacom, 1982.

Kirkpatrick, D. L. *No-Nonsense Communication.* (3rd ed.) Elm Grove, Wis.: Dr. Donald L. Kirkpatrick, 1983.

Kirkpatrick, D. L., Coverdale, D. S., and Olsen-Tjensvold, R. *How to Select and Train New First-Line Supervisors.* Chicago: Dartnell Corp., 1980.

Land, P. A. "Sir, I Assume Command." *Air University Review,* 1983, *34* (6), 20-28.

Likert, R. *The Human Organization.* New York: McGraw-Hill, 1967.

Lippitt, R. *Making Organizations Humane and Productive.* New York: Wiley, 1981.

Luthans, F., Maciag, W. S., and Rosenkrantz, S. A. "O.B. Mod: Meeting the Productivity Challenge with Human Resources Management." *Personnel,* Mar.-Apr. 1983, pp. 28-36.

McGregor, D. *The Human Side of Enterprise.* New York: McGraw-Hill, 1960.

Maier, N. R. F. *Problem-Solving Discussions and Conferences.* New York: McGraw-Hill, 1963.

Margulies, N., and Wallace, J. *Organization Change: Techniques and Application.* Glenview, Ill.: Scott, Foresman, 1973.

Marrow, A. J. *The Failure of Success.* New York: Amacom, 1972.

Mohr, W., and Mohr, H. *Quality Circles: Changing Images of People at Work.* Reading, Mass.: Addison-Wesley, 1983.

Myers, M. S. *Every Employee a Manager.* New York: McGraw-Hill, 1970.

Odiorne, G. *The Change Resisters.* Englewood Cliffs, N.J.: Prentice-Hall, 1981.

Oncken, W., and Wass, D. L. "Management Time: Who's Got the Monkey?" *Harvard Business Review,* Nov.-Dec. 1974, pp. 75-80.

"Overcoming Resistance to Change." Beverly Hills, Calif.: Roundtable Films, 1962.

Personnel, Nov.-Dec. 1958, pp. 16-39.

Plain Dealer, Cleveland, Ohio, October 17, 1983.

Rogers, E. M. *Diffusion of Innovations.* New York: Free Press, 1962.

Schaller, L. E. *The Change Agent.* Nashville, Tenn.: Abingdon Press, 1978.

Society for Advancement of Management, New York, American Management Associations, 1980.

Straits Times, Singapore, November 10, 1983.

Thomson, P. C. *Quality Circles—How to Make Them Work in America.* New York: Amacom, 1982.

Townsend, R. *Up the Organization.* New York: Fawcett World Library, 1970.

Tyre, T. E., and Bojar, J. A. "Behavioral Dentistry: New Techniques for the Management of the Anxious Dental Patient." *Journal of the Wisconsin Dental Association,* 1980, *56* (10), 633-635.

Wall Street Journal, January 25, 1984.

Index